SAVE THE PAST FOR THE FUTURE II: REPORT OF THE WORKING CONFERENCE

Breckenridge, Colorado
September 19–22, 1994

SAA

SOCIETY FOR AMERICAN ARCHAEOLOGY

Society for American Archaeology
900 Second St NE #12
Washington DC 20002-3557 USA
Tel: +1 202-789-8200
Fax: +1 202-789-0284

Save the Past for the Future II: Report of the Working Conference
ISBN 0-932839-13-4

The Society for American Archaeology thanks the following organizations for their support of the Save the Past for the Future II conference: Department of Defense Legacy Program, National Park Service (Rangers, Archeological Assistance Division, and Southeast Region), Bureau of Land Management, Bureau of Reclamation, Fish and Wildlife Service, Soil Conservation Service, American Association of Museums, Society for Historical Archaeology, and National Conference of State Historic Preservation Officers.

Save the Past for the Future II: Report of the Working Conference is distributed free to members of the Society for American Archaeology. Copies are also available for $5.00 plus $3 postage and handling by writing to SAA at the address above.

Cover design by Andrew Berman, Supon Design Group, Washington, D.C.

Printed by Allen Press, Lawrence, Kansas.

This publication has been printed on recycled paper.

CONTENTS

5 PREFACE
Bruce Smith

7 PLANNING COMMITTEE AND WORKSHOP CHAIRS

9 INTRODUCTION
William D. Lipe

OPENING SESSION

11 *Loretta Neumann*
CEHP Incorporated

15 *Mary C. Spearing*
Criminal Division, U.S. Department of Justice

19 *Michael Sweeney*
National Park Service, U.S. Department of the Interior

21 *Elizabeth Estill*
Forest Service, U.S. Department of Agriculture

23 *Susan Collins*
State Archaeologist, Colorado

25 *Brian Fagan*
University of California-Santa Barbara

WORKSHOPS

31 Education
George Smith, chair

41 Integrated Resource Management
Marilyn Nickels, chair

47 Law Enforcement
Robert Marriott, chair

53 PARTICIPANTS

PREFACE

BRUCE D. SMITH

ARCHAEOLOGY TODAY is a diverse discipline, providing a rich variety of career paths in government and the private sector, as well as in universities, museums, and other educational settings. Even though these career paths often lead off in very different directions, all archaeologists are united in sharing a deeply held dedication to protecting archaeological sites from looting.

For six decades the Society for American Archaeology has been involved in the ongoing struggle against the looting of archaeological sites on both private and public lands in the United States as well as in other countries of the Americas. In cooperation with the Instituto Nacional de Antropologia e Historia in Mexico, SAA will cosponsor a conference in 1996 in Mexico City on site protection in Latin America. Also scheduled, for 1995, is a National Park Service–supported workshop on protection of sites on private lands, cosponsored by SAA, the Archaeological Conservancy, the National Conference of State Historic Preservation Officers, the National Trust for Historic Preservation, and the Society for Historical Archaeology. These upcoming conferences, focused on Latin America and issues of site protection on private land, form a logical triad with the 1994 conference in Breckenridge, reported here, which addressed issues of site protection on public lands in the United States.

The Breckenridge conference, too, was a cooperative undertaking, reflecting a strengthening partnership between SAA and agencies of the federal government in the continuing fight against looting on public lands. Agencies of the departments of Agriculture, Defense, and Interior all contributed essential funding support for the conference, along with contributions from allied organizations, namely the American Association of Museums, the National Conference of State Historic Preservation Officers, and the Society for Historical Archaeology.

Just as important to the success of the Breckenridge conference was the contribution of time, energy, and expertise by archaeologists and resource managers from federal agencies, who played important roles in conference planning. I would like to thank the workshop chairs and all of the members of the planning committee (listed on page 5) for their ideas, insights, hard work and common commitment to making the conference a success.

During the spring and summer of 1994, the planning committee addressed a sequence of interrelated issues: sources of funding were identified and approached, budgets were developed, the location of the conference was selected, meeting formats and schedules were discussed and refined, workshop agendas were developed in cooperation with workshop chairs, and anticipated results were outlined. This report reflects the success of the Breckenridge conference in achieving impressive results in two of the three general goal areas identified by the planning committee, and outlines what is necessary in order to achieve the all-important third goal.

The first and most basic goal of the conference was to provide a structured forum to bring together 160 people from across the United States in order to assess progress made in combating archaeological looting over the last four years and to chart actions necessary in the future to continue hard-won gains. Participants were not only strongly dedicated to combating looting through education, law enforcement, and better management, but also were representative of several constituencies. By providing a common meeting ground, the Breckenridge conference helped to strengthen and reaffirm networks of communication and common purpose.

The second goal was to produce a battle plan—a set of interrelated objectives and strategies for improving site protection in the coming years. This report represents that battle plan, and reflects the impressive hard work and vision of all of the participants in the Breckenridge conference.

This report also defines the third and most important goal of the conference—the formidable challenge of carrying through on the battle plan, of undertaking the numerous initiatives outlined herein, and achieving the many goals that have been set out. This challenge—the most difficult—is now before us all.

Bruce D. Smith is president of the Society for American Archaeology. He is with the Department of Anthropology, American Museum of Natural History, Smithsonian Institution, Washington, D.C.

Planning Committee

Richard Brook
7Division of Cultural Heritage
Bureau of Land Management
U.S. Department of the Interior

Ed Friedman
Lands, Recreation, and Cultural Resources Branch
Bureau of Reclamation
U.S. Department of the Interior

Daniel Haas
Archeological Assistance Division
National Park Service
U. S. Department of the Interior

Ralph Johnson
Society for American Archaeology

Mike Kaczor
Economics and Social Sciences
Soil Conservation Service
U.S. Department of Agriculture

Kevin Kilcullen
Division of Refuges
Fish and Wildlife Service
U.S. Department of the Interior

William D. Lipe, *Conference chair*
Washington State University and
Crow Canyon Archaeological Center

Robert Marriott, *Law Enforcement Workshop chair*
Ranger Activities
National Park Service
U.S. Department of the Interior

Loretta Neumann
CEHP Incorporated

Marilyn Nickels, *Integrated Resource Management Workshop chair*
Division of Cultural Heritage
Bureau of Land Management
U.S. Department of the Interior

Jill Osborn
Heritage Programs
Forest Service
U.S. Department of Agriculture

Kathleen Schamel
CEHP Incorporated

Bruce Smith, *Planning Committee chair*
National Museum of Natural History
Smithsonian Institution

George Smith, *Education Workshop chair*
Southeast Archeological Center
National Park Service
U.S. Department of the Interior

Melanie Stright
Environmental Operations and Analysis
Minerals Management Service
U.S. Department of the Interior

Mimi Woods
Environmental Programs Directorate
U.S. Army

INTRODUCTION

WILLIAM D. LIPE

THE CONTINUING LOSS of archaeological sites due to vandalism, looting, and development threatens the core value of archaeology as a means for gaining new information about the past through systematic field research. These losses also strike at the valued roles that particular archaeological sites play in the heritage and living traditions of indigenous peoples and other cultural groups in the Americas. In May 1989 the first working conference, Save the Past for the Future, was convened at Taos, New Mexico, under SAA leadership. This conference focused the attention of archaeologists, agency resource managers, and law enforcement personnel on the critical status of the problem and produced an action plan for fighting vandalism and looting, embodied in the meeting's final report, *Save the Past for the Future: Actions for the '90s*.

In the little more than five years since the Taos conference, progress has been made on some fronts. Not all of it is directly attributable to the Taos conference, but that meeting was a catalyst, and a sign that many people in and out of the archaeological profession were ready to "do something." Since Taos, federal law enforcement and legal staffs have gained more experience in making and prosecuting cases under the Archeological Resources Protection Act, and the courts are beginning to take these cases more seriously. Archaeologists working in academic, agency resource management, contract research, and avocational contexts are more aware of the problem's magnitude and more willing to become engaged in addressing it. Native American tribes have become more active in archaeological resource protection on tribal lands, while the Native American Graves Protection and Repatriation Act and regulations regarding traditional cultural properties have given tribal heritage values much greater weight in archaeological resource management and protection on federal lands. Public education—about archaeology, culture history, and site protection—has literally exploded. One of the outcomes of the Taos conference was the formation of the SAA's Committee on Public Education, which now mails its newsletter to more than 6,000 people, a large number of whom are K–12 teachers.

Although the battle has been joined, it is not one that can ever really end—success will lie only in dramatically slowing the rate at which sites are being lost. To help develop strategy and tactics for continuing the campaign, 160 people met in Breckenridge, Colorado, on September 19–23, 1994. After the first evening's opening session—invigorated by Brian Fagan's powerful discussion of archaeology's value—and the next morning's brief plenary session spelling out the conference goals, the participants separated into three workshops, each meeting for two and a half days of intense effort, followed by a presentation of findings and recommendations at a final plenary session.

Workshops were organized around these themes: education, law enforcement, and integrated resource management. Reflecting now on what I learned at the conference, several aspects stand out.

First, I was impressed by the intensity and commitment of the participants. These people really worked, and their energy and enthusiasm were synergistic. I felt at the time that if that level of intensity could be maintained when the participants returned to their regular contexts, they would be able to inspire an army of recruits.

My second observation: they were going to have to recruit and inspire such an army if we were to work our way very far down the lists of action items the workshop leaders presented. These goals are in fact very ambitious, but they must be, given the size of the problem. If the time is right, and the energy is there, even an ambitious agenda can be successfully pursued.

Third, several of the workshops focused as much on what archaeology is good for, as on the specific problems of how to stop site loss.

The law enforcement people, of course, are right on the firing line, and properly stressed how to prevent and prosecute looting and vandalism. But both the education and integrated resource management workshops dealt with not only getting out messages about site protection, but also how archaeology can be made more relevant to a broader public. Thus, the educators emphasized ways in which Native American and other cultural histories can contribute richness and time depth to the public's understanding of America's roots. And the resource management workshop developed themes such as the "long view" of humans as active participants in ecosystems, and the value of archaeological research in understanding both natural and cultural factors in ecosystem evolution. I thought the conference reached an appropriate balance here. Surely we will not slow site loss without direct measures to enforce laws and make looting publicly unacceptable. But neither will we accomplish this effectively if more land managers, private land holders, and members of the general public do not come to see archaeology and archaeological sites as of current and future value in their own lives and work.

William D. Lipe, president-elect of the Society for American Archaeology, is with Washington State University, Pullman, and Crow Canyon Archaeological Center, Cortez, Colorado.

LOOKING BACK WHILE WE LOOK AHEAD

LORETTA NEUMANN

FIVE YEARS AGO, many of the people in this room met at the Fort Burgwin Research Center in Taos, New Mexico. Our purpose was to discuss the same issue that brought us here today—how to protect archaeological sites from looting and vandalism. For those who were with us in Taos, I can only say that it is great to see you again. But it is also great to see so many new faces of those who were not with us before. Such a gathering gives us the advantage of having "institutional knowledge"—a history to draw upon—as well as many fresh thoughts and new ideas.

I have been asked to give a brief history on the background of this conference. My history lesson actually starts nearly a hundred years ago. Because of the looting of sites in the southwestern states at the turn of the nineteenth century, the United States Congress passed the Antiquities Act of 1906. The purpose was to protect sites on federally owned lands. The Antiquities Act requires permits for excavations and provided penalties for damaging historic or prehistoric ruins. It also gives the president power to set aside as national monuments areas of public land with historic and prehistoric values. Other statutes were enacted over the years to protect historical and archaeological sites. These include the Historic Sites Act, the National Historic Preservation Act, the Archaeological Resources Protection Act (ARPA), Abandoned Shipwrecks Act, and, most recently, the Native American Graves Protection and Repatriation Act (NAGPRA).

I have had the privilege of working on most of these statutes for the past 20 years, first as a professional staff member for the U.S. House of Representatives and now as a private consultant. This experience has taught me some key principles about federal laws. They are not self actuating. They often take as much or more work to get implemented as they took to get enacted. They usually start as an effort to solve a real or perceived problem. Yet they seldom are perfect. Today's solution may actually cause tomorrow's problem. Or, at the least, something important may have been overlooked and need to be included or corrected later.

ARPA is a case in point. It became needed because a federal court held, during the 1970s, that the definition of artifact under the Antiquities Act was unconstitutionally vague. The Society for American Archaeology (SAA) took the lead in developing and promoting passage of new legislation to remedy this problem. I remember Dr. Raymond Thompson, then president of SAA, coming to visit our congressional offices. He brought SAA's first paid lobbyist with him, Mark Michael, who now heads the Archaeological Conservancy. They worked very hard for the passage of ARPA. It was a tough battle. The legislation finally passed in 1979. As enacted, ARPA regulates the taking of archaeological resources on federal lands. It requires a permit system for excavating or removing archaeological resources and prohibits the sale, purchase, transport or entry into interstate commerce of items taken in violation of the Act. Civil and criminal penalties are provided.

But, as I mentioned, laws are not self actuating. Even after passage of ARPA, it took the National Park Service five years to get regulations in place. In 1987 the General Accounting Office published a report documenting for the first time the ineffectiveness of ARPA. It told in graphic terms the increasing destruction of sites on federal lands. This was followed in early 1988 with a report by a subcommittee of the House of Representatives. This report further described the looting and vandalism of archaeological sites in the Four Corners states of the Southwest. These reports, and other information gathered at the time, documented problems with ARPA. The act was very difficult to enforce. The threshold for a felony conviction was $5,000 damage, a sum that was too high and difficult to estimate or prove. Also, a person could not be convicted unless he or she got caught in the act—obviously something not always possible to do.

As a result, SAA again took the lead to get ARPA amended. By "whiting out" a zero, we got the threshold lowered to $500. And by inserting a few clever and much-needed words, the act now includes the "attempt" to damage a site, making it easier to prosecute violators.

Although we got these amendments enacted in 1988, we learned a great deal in the process: Namely, many problems remained to be solved, and many more issues needed to be addressed. Not everything could be helped by passing a law. We lacked understanding of why some people loot and others don't. Much damage is done to archaeological sites by the inadvertent taking of artifacts by well-meaning people. We also found that law enforcement officers and prosecutors lacked training and support. Juries were unwilling to convict because they, as well as many other members of the general public, often didn't view this as a crime.

Several of us who had worked so hard on these issues believed that much more needed to be done. We felt strongly that it would only get done if the profession itself took the initiative. Hence in 1988, Kathleen (Reinburg) Schamel and I put together a proposal for an SAA sponsored project that would bring together the affected federal agencies and other stakeholders to look at the whole picture, not just the laws. This led to the Save the Past for the Future project. The project had many components, including several symposia and other sessions at SAA annual meetings. Critical to its success was the formation of a steering committee, composed of representatives of the participating agencies and organizations. Annetta Cheek, a past officer of SAA, chaired it. Our frequent meetings helped us frame the issues and find ways to be supportive. I regreted when it ended.

A new committee, fortunately, was established to prepare for this conference at Breckenridge, chaired by Bruce Smith, the current president of SAA. I do hope that it can remain in existence after the conference to help ensure that the recommendations get implemented.

One of the high points of the original project was, in fact, the Taos conference, which was directed by James Judge. This very intense week of work resulted in a report, *Save the Past for the Future: Actions for the '90s*. That report is still very relevant. Many of its recommendations have been implemented. Many more await action.

Most important, the report gave us something to rally around. We used it to lobby Congress for more funding, and we got it—not the least of which was annual earmarked funds for NPS law enforcement, which continue today. It also resulted in increased attention to the issue in the other land managing agencies such as the Forest Service, Bureau of Land Management (BLM) and the Fish and Wildlife Service (FWS). It also led to the formation of SAA's Public Education Committee, chaired by Ed Friedman. The BLM produced many fine public service announcements. The Forest Service expanded its fine Passport in Time program. Many interagency efforts have gotten under way, including several that involve the Justice Department.

Despite all of this, protecting sites is still an issue. Funding remains a critical problem. The Forest Service is facing a dramatic cut in its funds for cultural resource management. The FWS and BLM have never been sufficiently funded. The current administration's efforts to reinvent government may have some devastating effects on BLM's ability to carry out its cultural resource responsibilities.

Concern is also growing about the destruction of archaeological resources in other countries. Currently, for example, the Clinton administration is planning to propose ratification of the Hague Convention for the protection of cultural properties during times of armed conflict. This could be a very important tool for protecting sites in peacetime as well, since it requires participating countries to take a number of actions in order to inventory and designate their cultural treasures, including archaeological sites.

Meanwhile, new programs have begun—ecosystem management, biodiversity, sustainable development, heritage areas. These show great promise. Yet cultural resources do not appear prominently among them. We have failed to make much of a case with biologists and others in the government that cultural resources and archaeological site protection is part of their mission.

The public, despite our many efforts at outreach, still lacks awareness, even those who are highly educated. An example is in your conference notebook, an article I read in the Environmental Defense Fund newsletter. It's about a biologist who is very proud of his collecting prehistoric Native American artifacts. He says he is careful to collect from disturbed sites (such as farm fields) and to register all finds. He hopes eventually to publish a technical monograph on the subject. How should we respond to him?

That is why we are here today. To look at these issues—old and new—with fresh eyes. To see what has worked and what has not. To review what has been done and what remains to be done.

Before closing this history lesson, I want to acknowledge some people who are here and some who are not. All have been very helpful over the past six years. I have already named a few. Here are some more:

- Former SAA presidents Dina Dincauze and Jerry Sabloff, under whose terms the original project was conducted and who were both very helpful. Also Cheryl Munson, who chaired the SAA Government Affairs Committee and whose passion for the looting issue kept it alive.
- Philip Speser, my predecessor as the Washington representative for SAA, who was very supportive of our original project ideas.
- Leslie Wildeson, who helped edit the *Actions for the '90s* report. Also Frank McManamon of the National Park Service, who had the foresight to order extra copies

of it and gave them back to us so we could have them here today. And George Smith of the NPS whose enthusiasm and energy kept us and still keeps us in good spirits, no matter how long the hours nor how hard the work.

• The chairs of the Taos workshops, Sherri Lerner, Martin McAllister, and Chris Christensen. They did an amazingly effective job of building consensus. And Tom King, who did an extensive amount of research and made a fine presentation at the first SAA symposium on the topic of looting.

• Judge Sherry Hutt, who has given an enormous amount of her personal time to help promote training of law enforcement officials. And Bob Marriott, who has made the National Park Service law enforcement program so effective.

• Richard Brook of the BLM and Kevin Kilcullen of the FWS, who worked so hard both on the Taos conference and on this one. Unfortunately, neither can be here because of unforeseen circumstances. We do miss them.

• Elizabeth Estill, then the Forest Service's director of recreation, wilderness, and cultural resources and now the Rocky Mountain regional forester, who was extremely supportive in helping us launch the Save the Past for the Future project.

These are people who helped five years ago, most of whom are still very active in these issues, some of whom are with us today. I would also like to acknowledge the CEHP staff who have handled the logistics for this conference—Paul Hallam and Jill Schaefer. Of course, Kathleen Schamel, who has worked extremely hard and cheerfully on both conferences. Also, many, many thanks to the sponsors of this conference today, who gave both money and much in-kind support to make it happen.

Lastly, many thanks to ***all*** of you for coming. What we are doing is important. The past may be prologue, but the present is here. And right now we have the chance to work together to make the future even better.

Loretta Neumann is president of CEHP (Conservation, Environment, and Historic Preservation) Incorporated, in Washington, D.C.

REMARKS

MARY C. SPEARING

THANK YOU, DR. LIPE, for your very gracious remarks. Jo Ann Harris, the assistant attorney general for the Criminal Division, wanted to be with you today, but unfortunately has a conflicting obligation to testify before a congressional committee.

Ms. Harris has a very personal interest in archeological protection; she is an amateur archeologist who has participated in archeological digging, related to her interest is prehistoric North America, in the United States, and Siberia.

As section chief of the General Litigation and Legal Advice Section, the component of the Criminal Division responsible for coordinating and providing legal advice and assistance for overseeing the enforcement of the Archaeological Resources Protection Act, it is my pleasure to provide some brief comments regarding "Current issues in archeological protection for the Department of Justice."

This is an exciting time for all of us who are concerned about the protection of the richly varied archeological resources which constitute part of the treasure of our history and prehistory in the United States. Since the enactment of the Archaeological Resources Protection Act of 1979 (ARPA) [16 U.S.C. §470aa et seq.] and the more recent enactment of the Native American Graves Protection and Repatriation Act of 1990 (NAGPRA), a portion of which is codified as the Illegal Trafficking in Native American Human Remains and Cultural Items Act [18 U.S.C. §1170], we now have tools that, if utilized properly—in a criminal, civil, or administrative context or some combination thereof—can be an effective deterrent in preventing further destruction of our archeological and cultural resources.

The congressional findings and declaration of purpose set out in the Archaeological Resources Protection Act state:

> archeological resources on public lands and Indian lands are an accessible and irreplaceable part of the Nation's heritage;
> these resources are increasingly endangered because of their commercial attractiveness; and that
> existing Federal laws do not provide adequate protection to prevent the loss and destruction of these archaeological resources and sites resulting from uncontrolled excavations and pillage. [16 U.S.C. §470aa, (a)(1), (2) and (3)].

The purpose of the statute as stated in the statute (§470aa, (b)] is to secure, for the present and future benefit of the American people, the protection of archeological resources and sites that are on public lands and Indian lands, and to foster increased cooperation and exchange of information between governmental authorities, the professional archeological community, and private individuals having collections of archeological resources.

These findings and declaration of purpose are, of course, correct in saying that these resources are an irreplaceable part of our heritage and that protecting our archeological resources is for the present and future benefit of the American people. But the preservation of these resources is more than a benefit to our society; it is a necessity and of vital importance to every individual. The preservation and protection of historical and archeological resources involves more than artifacts, battlefields, and other tangible items. What we are actually protecting are the values, beliefs, and aspiration of people that are passed from generation to generation. Our lives and the lives of those who came before us are given meaning and significance because cultural values, universal principles of freedom and liberty, are shared with others now and in the future.

For these cultural treasures of values and beliefs to be passed on to the next generation and generations far in the future we must be ever alert to protecting our historical resources so that we can search for the truth of our past and derive its meaning.

Our recollections of the past enable us to see more clearly the meaning of the present. By protecting archeological resources through law enforcement we are not only preserving those sites for a greater understanding of our history, but we are enabling ourselves to tell an unfinished story to an ever widening public. The looting and destruction of historical sites cannot be permitted to overwhelm the public's need to understand its history and to feel a closeness with the cultural values of those who preceded us. A reverence for the past and a willingness to extend our efforts in preservation and protection of historical resources will shine a wider light on our understanding of our present society. Our recollections of the past enable us to see more clearly the meaning of the present.

The Department of Justice is an important component in the cooperative effort to preserve and protect historical resources. A recent Supreme Court decision confirmed the availability of criminal justice resources for archeological protection efforts. On January 18, 1994, the United States Supreme Court denied certiorari in an important case construing a key provision of the Archaeological Resources Protection Act. In *United States v. Gerber*[1], Judge Posner of the Seventh Circuit Court of Appeals held, for a unanimous court, that the ARPA was *not* limited to archeological objects removed from federal and Indian lands but that is also applied, in certain circumstances, to the removal of archeological resources from private property without the owner's permission.

In *Gerber* the "Indian relic" predators, without permission, entered upon land in Indiana owned by the General Electric Company, and in a manner that constituted criminal conversion and criminal trespass under Indiana state law, excavated and removed numerous prehistoric artifacts from an ancient burial mound affiliated with the "Hopewell phenomenon" culture. This "GE Mound" in southwestern Indiana was one of the five largest known Hopewell burial mounds. Gerber and his cohorts tore it apart. I do not need to tell you of the magnitude of the loss resulting from that kind of destructive plundering. The case was successfully prosecuted by the United States Attorney's Office for the Southern District of Indiana.

The lead defendant, Arthur Gerber, was sentenced in July 1992 to 12 months imprisonment followed by three years' supervised release, in addition to a $5,000 fine, a $125 special assessment, and a $4,750 forfeiture. Gerber was also ordered not to sell, purchase, barter, or excavate any archeological resources, or to sponsor, organize, or attend any shows or exhibitions that have any archeological resources exhibited. Gerber began serving his term of imprisonment at the Fort Worth Federal Correctional Institution in May 1994. His four associates were all sentenced to two years probation with the condition that they serve specified periods of either work release or home detention ranging from 30 days to 180 days. Two of those associates were also fined $2,000 and $5,000, respectively. They also began to serve their sentences in May 1994.

The *Gerber* case, in combination with *United States v. Austin*[2], a decision of the Ninth Circuit Court of Appeals, which upheld the constitutionality of ARPA, provides a sound legal basis for successful criminal prosecutions under ARPA. Given this current state of the law, we see no sound legal reason for not prosecuting appropriate ARPA violations, even when they occur on private property.

Historically, almost all criminal ARPA offenses have been investigated by agents and archeologists employed by the respective federal agency with responsibility over the land on which the unlawful excavation and removal occurred, with the Federal Bureau of Investigation being called in to assist, if requested, in major investigations or when no federal land managing agency has jurisdiction—as was the case in the *Gerber* prosecutions. Any subsequent federal prosecution is then pursued by the responsible United States attorney's office, with legal assistance provided, if requested, by attorneys of the Criminal Division of the Department of Justice.

A paramount interest of the Department of Justice is ensuring that there are sufficient assistant United States attorneys located throughout the country who are versed in the various technical requirements of ARPA and other criminal and civil provisions that can be used to prosecute archeological resource violations, such as the theft of government property statute [18 U.S.C. §641] and the depredation of government property statute [18 U.S.C. §1361]. To this end, Department of Justice Criminal Division attorneys respond to inquiries, prepare reference materials for federal prosecutors, and conduct ongoing training programs for federal prosecutors.

Attorneys in my section and in our division's Asset Forfeiture Office are available to respond to any criminal or forfeiture matter inquiry by any assistant United States attorney, or attorney, investigator, archeologist, or other employee of any federal agency involved with archeological protection enforcement activities.

In 1992 Criminal Division attorneys, in conjunction with the National Park Service's Archeological Assistance Division and other members of the Interagency Archeological Protection Working Group, prepared a two-volume, loose-leaf publication entitled "Archeological Resources Protection: Federal Prosecution Sourcebook." This sourcebook has been distributed to all 94 United States attorney offices. In addition, the Archeological Assistance Division has distributed the sourcebook to a wide variety of agency attorneys, land managers, archeologists, criminal investigators, and Indian tribal leaders. We feel that this sourcebook, which is supplemented annually, is a valuable training tool, which further educates its users and eventually will lead to more ARPA prosecutions.

Criminal Division attorneys, in association with the Archeological Assistance Division and the Executive Office of United States Attorneys of the Department of Justice, participate in an annual two-day conference entitled Overview of Archeological Protection Law. The conference is cosponsored by the Archeological Assistance Division and the Department of Justice. This conference has provided intensive training to more than 40 assistant United States attorneys, in addition to a number of agency personnel and other individuals involved in the preservation of our rich archeological heritage.

Historical preservation permits us to gain a better understanding of ourselves—the value systems, beliefs, concepts, outlooks, and even mistaken judgments of those who came before us are responsible in large part for the lives we now lead. Only through a clear vision of the past and creatively using our understanding of the past can we expect to make a better life for future generations. The Department of Justice is pleased to join you as an active participant in archeological protection cooperative efforts.

Thank you for the chance to present these short remarks. I look forward to working with you to help protect our archeological resources.

Mary Spearing is chief of the General Litigation and Legal Advice Section, Criminal Division, Department of Justice, Washington, D.C.

REMARKS

MICHAEL SWEENEY

I'D LIKE TO BEGIN by extending Assistant Secretary Bonnie Cohen's apologies for not being able to be here today. Unfortunately, or fortunately, I guess, depending on how you look at it, she had to be in Cancun for a meeting on environmental issues related to NAFTA. At any rate, Bonnie asked me to make some remarks in her absence on behalf of the Department of the Interior. In light of our work and your interest in ecosystem management, she asked me to talk about this approach specifically as it relates to cultural resources.

As you know, "ecosystem management" has virtually become the new mantra of the federal land managing agencies. You will be discussing the substance of this turn here under the title "integrated resources management," which is a bit longer but perhaps describes better what this approach in general is all about.

After years of addressing the protection of endangered and threatened species piecemeal, animal by animal and plant by plant, the land managing agencies are coming to realize that, in doing so, they were faced with the often Sisyphean task of protecting one species only to see another threatened nearby. The crisis in the Pacific Northwest, for example, was promising to become a problem of not one species but over 400. Ecosystem management is one solution currently being hammered out that seeks to move beyond the single-species approach to a focus on the entire web of species, including people, that comprises an ecosystem and on the larger problems and trends that affect their long-term health and survival as a whole.

Similarly, there is now a growing understanding of the need to take account of the cultural and historic landscape as part of the new ecosystem or "integrated" approach to land management, which considers a host of factors that shape and have shaped the land.

History is part of the landscape, both figuratively and physically, and an area's ecology is by no means a static attribute, but one that has evolved over time and continues to evolve, often due, far better or far worse, to the activities of people and their civilizations. Cultural resources can be key to understanding the long-term trends that have created today's environment. Archaeological sites, for example, can be time capsules not only of human culture, but also of ecologies past in the form of fossilized pollen, animal bones, seeds, and other organic remains.

Apart from ensuring that ecosystem management efforts take into consideration cultural resources, however, it is also valuable to take an integrated approach to cultural resources in their own right. It seems critical to study and to interpret for people the relationships between cultural resources on, and off, the map, to paint a picture of a historic landscape to which both managers and the public can relate.

Integrating the management of cultural and natural resources and drawing connections between the pieces of our cultural heritage strewn across the landscape are among the goals of the National Park Service's Heritage Partnerships initiative. This concept acknowledges the all-important fact that "integrated" means fostering partnerships between federal, state, and local and private entities—all the stakeholders—to achieve conservation goals alongside healthy economies.

Finally, perhaps the most important word here is "local," that is conservation from the bottom up—the only kind that will ensure the long-term viability of success. But, so often, as you all know, people aren't sufficiently aware of their cultural or natural heritage to want or care to protect it. Education, therefore, as in so many efforts, is the cornerstone of conservation, for, as Aldo Leopold wrote, "When we see the land as a community to which we belong, we may begin to use it with love and respect."

Thank you or allowing me to speak to you today. This is a very exciting subject, and I'm sure we'll have a productive week.

Michael Sweeney is special assistant in the Office of the Secretary of the Interior, U.S. Department of the Interior, Washington, D.C.

REMARKS

ELIZABETH ESTILL

THIS CONFERENCE REPRESENTS the integration we keep talking about in the federal land managing agencies—integration where players from many backgrounds come together to focus on a single issue. Protection of our nation's heritage is of vital importance, not just to historic preservation professionals, but to all land managers, to indigenous peoples, and to future generations. Archaeologists, historians, educators, land managers, native people, law enforcement and judicial experts from the public and private sectors all need to be involved if protection efforts are to work. This conference is a unique gathering of all those individuals. You have before you a monumental task, one with many challenges, but one with many rewards too. An effective protection program will guarantee not only survival of valuable heritage sites for our children and grandchildren to enjoy, but recovery of environmental and human use information that will guide our management of natural resources, and protection of traditional ways of life.

You have divided yourselves up into three working groups: public education, law enforcement, and ecosystem management. When I think of these three topics in the context of protection of heritage resources, many things come to mind that I hope you will address this week.

Five years ago, Taos conference attendees recognized that unless the public knew what archaeology was and why it was important, we couldn't hope to combat the large-scale looting of sites. Out of this emphasis on education grew such successful programs as the National Register's Teaching with Historic Places, the Forest Service's Passport in Time, BLM's Adventures in the Past, and a host of others. There are now many ways the public can become involved. Your efforts at Taos and since have been wildly successful in initiating these public education programs. The battle for recognition of the value of public education has been won. Now we must focus on what kinds of educational programs are the most effective and how we can best meet the needs of our rapidly changing and increasingly educated and involved publics.

From the federal agency perspective I hope you will find some time to focus on two concepts with regard to public education: integration of heritage education into environmental and conservation education and the role of stewardship or involvement in research and management as an education tool. Heritage interpretation should not be separate from environmental and conservation education. As anthropologists, you study people in the context of their natural and cultural environments. Anthropologists are those who can show us how people affected the natural resources and, in turn, how resources shaped cultures. The relationship between humans and their environment is what ecosystem management is all about.

And you are lucky, because what you study is something the public finds irresistibly interesting. Archaeology is a natural for public stewardship—a powerful education tool. Programs where the public actually assists with research and management are very effective, not to mention very popular. Today's highly educated, highly motivated public doesn't just want to be fed results, they want to be involved in the process. Think beyond the traditional educational boxes. Involvement is the key to the Baby Boomers' hearts!

No matter how good our education programs are, we will always need law enforcement. Five years ago, one of our biggest challenges was to educate the district attorneys and judges so they would begin to try ARPA cases. Through your efforts you were able to raise the awareness of many within the legal and judicial system. Now, five years and many successful prosecutions later, we need to discuss how to keep the momentum going, especially in the face of broad-scale reorganization of federal agencies with the responsibility of protecting many resources. How can we ensure that enforcement efforts cross jurisdictional lines? How can we improve training for those involved in ARPA cases? How can we more effectively communicate case results among agencies and organizations? How can we integrate protection of the archaeological resources with other resource protection efforts? These are some of the questions I hope you tackle this week.

And finally, I am glad to see that you will discuss ecosystem management. If we cannot show that archaeological sites contain data relevant in making land management decisions affecting resources that people depend on and have depended on for thousands of years, then we should all go home. We must show that the archaeological record is not just about the "human dimension" of ecosystem management. It is about cultural ecology; it is about paleobotanical data; it is about geomorphological data; it will show us cycles of drought and deluge; it will show us indigenous crops that have since disappeared, and it might tell us why they disappeared. Through this discussion, we should be able to tell managers that they lose much more than a "neat old site" when they lose an archaeological site; they lose information that could have helped them make better land management decisions—for resources and for people. This workshop should be a context for the other two. It should chart a way to integrate archaeological protection and education efforts into ecosystem protection and environmental/conservation education.

This brings me to my closing thought. This conference should be about integration: integration of archaeological data into ecosystem management; integration of heritage education into environmental and conservation education; integration of site protection into ecosystem protection; and integration of all your collective talents, professions, and responsibilities, into the single passion for interpreting and protecting this nation's cultural heritage.

Elizabeth Estill is regional forester with the U.S. Department of Agriculture's Forest Service, Rocky Mountain Region.

PROGRESS IN PRESERVATION

SUSAN COLLINS

ON BEHALF OF the people of Colorado, I welcome you to our state. Several of you have already commented on the beauty of this country, and I encourage you to take some time to enjoy the scenery around us. Please take a Colorado Archaeology Preservation Week poster, which doubles as a guide to archaeological sites open to the public. This guide was written by Bill Butler of the National Park Service. While welcoming visitors, I'd also like to acknowledge in-state colleagues, especially those who serve on the Colorado Interagency Anti-Vandalism Task Force. Thank you for your work.

We are all looking forward to this conference with anticipation. There has been progress in the five years since the first Save the Past for the Future conference was held, in 1989, in Taos, New Mexico, to focus on preventing archaeological looting. The 1989 conference developed seven findings, with appropriate strategies:

- Information must reach the public;
- Education and training must be improved;
- Laws must be strengthened;
- Protection efforts must be increased;
- Agencies must improve coordination;
- More research on looting behavior is needed;
- Public participation must be provided.

These issues are being addressed. At the nationwide level, the National Historic Preservation Act has been strengthened, and the Native American Graves Protection and Repatriation Act passed. The Society for American Archaeology has developed a vigorous Public Education Committee, with the *Archaeology and Public Education* newsletter and communication networks in many states. Most states have strengthened their archaeology laws, particularly with regard to protection of burials on both private and public lands. Twenty-two states have annual archaeology weeks for community outreach. While hard data on the scope of vandalism and looting are notoriously hard to acquire, statements from both law enforcement officials and reformed diggers suggest that the battle is not lost.

I wish us well this week, as we work toward improved archaeological preservation nationwide.

Susan Collins is state archaeologist for Colorado.

PERHAPS WE MAY HEAR VOICES....

BRIAN M. FAGAN

TEN YEARS AGO, I stood at sunset atop a deep shell midden on a low cliff overlooking the Santa Barbara Channel. The setting sun painted the Pacific a deep pink, the ocean like a mirror in the calm evening.

I closed my eyes, listened to the lapping of the surf on the sand below. For a moment, the past flooded into my consciousness—a Chumash canoe easing through the surf, men and women grasping the gunwales with soft cries of welcome. Dogs barked, wood smoke drifted in the air, children played, as a shaman chanted softly... Just for a moment, the voices of the past drifted across the centuries into my consciousness.

That evening, I realized once again why I was an archaeologist, and why people are so fascinated by our discipline. The great Finnish paleontologist Bjorn Kurten once wrote: "None of the dead can rise up and answer our questions. But from all they have left behind, their imperishable or slowly dissolving gear, we may perhaps hear voices, which are only now able to whisper, when everything else has become silent" (Kurten, 1984).

A month ago, I visited the same spot on another gleaming summer's evening, hoping to relive the moment. All I found was a scarred battlefield of looters' pits and shredded spoil heaps. The voices had vanished into oblivion. It was then I finally realized that my grandchildren and great grandchildren may never listen to the voices of the past.

Archaeology—glittering gold and fabulous treasure, spectacular royal tombs, lost civilizations dimly visible through swirling mists.

- Unexplained mysteries, mother goddesses, the fabled power of ancient pyramids.
- Projectile points littering the surface of a plowed field picked up on a hot summer's day,
- Mimbres bowls gleaming seductively in a New York dealer's showroom.
- Spectacular discoveries made by pith-helmeted professors in distant lands, by men and women more adventurers than archaeologists.
- Scientists in white coats peering through microscopes looking at tiny seeds and discoursing wisely about artifacts and food remains.

Today's public is more sophisticated, better educated, and far more inquisitive. Yet the old stereotypes of archaeology and archaeologists linger. We are still seen as romantic adventurers as much as scientists. And many people still consider the rapidly vanishing archaeological record as some kind of private game reserve to be exploited and destroyed for fun and profit. The future of the past depends on changing these enduring attitudes. This conference comes five years after the first Save the Past for the Future meeting. It is time to assess what we have accomplished, to refine our role as stewards of the past. The conference workshops and sessions will explore such issues as public education, resource management, and law enforcement. But I think we need to ponder a very fundamental question, too. Why are archaeology and the remote past important to humankind? Why should we care about the voices of the past? Astonishing although it may seem, there is virtually no academic literature on this most basic of questions. One of the best statements on the subject was written as long ago as 1937 (Clark, 1937)! Much of this academic debate will revolve around different perspectives on the past: "And God said 'let us create man in our own image, after our likeness: and let them have dominion over the fish of the sea, and over the cattle, and over all the earth....'"

"Long ago there were no stars, no moon, and no sun. There was only darkness and water. A raft floated on the water and on the raft sat a turtle. Then from the sky a spirit came down and sat on the raft. Then the spirit said that something else was needed and he made people...."

Science tells us that the human past extends back more than 2.5 million years, into a world unimaginably different from our own. We scientists have a linear view of time, of human existence. To us, archaeological sites are a unique record of human achievement in every corner of the globe. They are the archives of the past, to be preserved as part of the collective cultural legacy of all humankind.

But many people define the world in very different terms. Many believe in the literal historical truth of Genesis, chapter 1, as a matter of Christian faith. Others, including many Native Americans, look at human existence in cyclical terms, participate in a spiritual world defined by the eternal verities of life and death, planting and harvest, sunset and sunrise. They believe that archaeology has no redeeming value, that the world of the ancestors is sacred, and to be left alone. Many Native Americans consider archaeology unnecessary, an unwarranted intrusion into their lives, their world, their history. But they have common cause with archaeologists in preserving sacred places, burial sites, and the settlements of the ancestors intact.

So we are all stewards of the past, scientists because the archaeological record is a chronicle of human existence, Native Americans for profound spiritual reasons.

Why is archaeology important? Because it is a lasting chronicle of thousands of years of extraordinary human achievement. Our remote ancestors survived the dramatic shifts of the Great Ice Age. They settled in harsh deserts and on arctic tundra, navigated the open waters of the Pacific Ocean more than 25,000 years ago. They domesticated cereal grasses, tamed animals, forged powerful chiefdoms and built great earthworks, living within, changing, and modifying the world's many environments.

It matters not that some of these ancestors were Native Americans, others Siberians, Chinese, Africans, or Europeans. As biologist Stephen J. Gould has pointed out, we are all products of a single African twig, all one humanity. And the only way we can understand this humanity is to comprehend its extraordinary evolution over more than 2.5 million years.

The archaeological record of North America, in all its remarkable diversity, however spectacular, however humble, is part of this common historical legacy. This is the legacy which is vanishing around us. This is the legacy we must preserve not just for a few generations, but for future millennia, simply because it will tell us more about ourselves, not necessarily today, but at some point in the future, too.

Perhaps most important of all, archaeology is about respect for diversity, for others. We are in the business not of educating people about archaeology, but about teaching them respect for other cultures and all of our past.

Last year, I spent two days at Wanuskewin, Canada, where archaeologists and Native Americans have cooperated in developing a magnificent interpretative center close to the North Saskatchewan River. The symbolic tepees of the center stand atop a small, pristine valley, where you explore the Plains environment of centuries, millennia ago. I walked through the valley, experiencing the subtle diversity of the local environment, learning how ancient visitors exploited its changing resources throughout the year. I talked with the Blackfoot and Cree men and women, who run the center, explored exhibits so realistic the computerized sound track evokes the savagery of a thunderstorm, the calm serenity of a snow-clad landscape.

Wanuskewin is not about archaeology, although archaeology is very much part of the picture. It is about respect for other cultures, ancient and modern. Wanuskewin tells of others' world views and cultural values.

Archaeology is important because it inculcates respect for other cultures, other people. The Canadians call this "heritage." I think we American archaeologists need to spend a lot of time thinking about the issue of heritage, about cultural diversity, and respect. The reasons why many Americans do not respect the archaeological record go far beyond mere greed and the lust to own artifacts. They do not consider it part of their history, a history perceived to begin with Christopher Columbus and the Pilgrim Fathers. What utter, ethnocentric nonsense! The world has moved on, our nation changed beyond all recognition. But our social attitudes toward the first chapter of our collective history are often fossilized in the historical attitudes of the 1950s. It is not enough to make people interested in archaeology. What we must inculcate in them is a respect for other cultures, their achievements and values. In this way the Paleoindian projectile point, the Pueblo painted pot, and the Hopewell mica ornament achieve a meaning far more than merely one of dollars and cents, of personal gain. All too often, even archaeologists themselves call such objects just "artifacts." We have forgotten they are the voices of the past, voices with an important message of respect to tell.

Archaeology is unique because it examines human behavior over long periods of time. I once stood on the shores of the Bering Strait on an early summer's day. I gazed across toward Siberia, over a gray landscape of heaving water and scattered ice floes. Then I remembered that the gloomy, windswept strait had been dry land a mere 12,000 years ago. I remembered what we know about it—a low-lying, windy place, rolling plains covered with stunted scrub extending to the far horizon. Only a few shallow river valleys offered shelter to animal and human alike. As I shivered in the chill wind, I pondered just how much North America has changed since then. The North American world of even 12,000 years ago was very different from our own. Vast ice sheets covered almost all of Canada. The Great Lakes did not exist. Extensive continental shelves extended far out from Atlantic, Gulf, and Pacific shores.

Six thousand years ago, the ice sheets were gone, ocean sea levels were at near-modern heights, hundreds of Ice Age big-game species were long extinct. The west was much drier than it had been for thousands of years.

Three thousand years ago, North America was environmentally very similar to what it was when the first Europeans arrived.

All this before Europeans changed the face of North America beyond all environmental recognition.

We live in a time of environmental crisis, of global warming, and massive human exploitation of our ecosystems. Scientists use sophisticated instruments to measure ancient climatic change deep beneath the Greenland ice sheet, study tree-rings and pollen diagrams to monitor drought cycles and long-term climatic change. Instruments tell us a great deal, but they are not human beings. Today, archaeology is a sophisticated, multidisciplinary science, which studies human interactions with the natural environment over both long and short periods of time. Archaeology is a vital part of modern, multidisciplinary environmental science, because it studies human behavior in the past.

How have humans coped with constant climatic change, with sudden cold snaps or prolonged drought cycles? How did they adapt crops to extremes of heat or arid lands? What were the environmental effects of forest clearance resulting from maize cultivation in the Mississippi Valley 2,000 years ago? Only archaeology and archaeological sites can tell us. To understand ourselves and our world, we must think of the archaeological record, and manage it as part of the ecosystem.

We talk about changing public attitudes to archaeology and the past, but we have hardly begun. I am simply astounded that there is virtually no scholarly literature which addresses the role of North American archaeology in the contemporary world. How can we change fundamental social attitudes to archaeology without serious scholarly consideration of the basics? How can we talk about the right of people to preserve their past, when we archaeologists have barely considered these issues in our own scholarly deliberations.

Make no mistake: the stakes are high. The future of archaeology is at issue. One hears of cutbacks on every side. I wager many of them result from sheer ignorance, from perceptions that archaeology is an idle luxury.

What nonsense! What myopia! And it is largely our fault if people believe archaeology is disposable. The 1990s are the moment of truth, the dawning of a fundamental sea change in the way in which archaeologists think and go about their business. No longer can one draw a line between academic researchers, subject to the stringent, narrow-minded "publish or perish" value system, and "professionals," concerned with management and conservation of the past. We are all in the same archaeological ark, adrift on stormy and uncertain seas, simply because our finite archives are vanishing before our eyes.

Perhaps the most important legacy of the 1989 Save the Past for the Future conference was an emerging debate about priorities, which pits the academic establishment with its concerns for scholarly knowledge against those many archaeologists who know that time is running out for the past. It is a debate not about knowledge, but about priorities, scarce research funds, and about education. This far-from-academic controversy will be ferocious and explosive, for the sea change in our discipline will have consequences far beyond the narrow world of archaeology. The debate will revolve around new generations of research, about conservation and the training of professionals, about changing social attitudes toward the past.

The archaeology of 2010 will be very different from that of 1994, one in which the conservation ethic, the issue of stewardship, will be all-pervasive. Yet we are unprepared:

- How many undergraduate and graduate archaeology curricula place conservation, ethics, and the value of the past at the very center of their curricula? How much attention have we given in our teaching to the notion that conservation begins with local communities, local people feeling strongly about their environment and the people who once lived in it (Marquardt, 1994).

- How many graduate programs combine rigorous academics with professional training in stewardship and public education? How many are preparing the next generations of archaeologists for the realities of a new archaeological world, where preservation of the finite resource on a global basis is our overwhelming priority?

- How can a genuinely new archaeology concerned with conservation and stewardship above all else flourish in an educational environment that values "publish or perish." Is archaeology unique as an academic discipline in its urgent need to make conservation and related activities as high a priority as conventional research. Does the Society for American Archaeology need to take a leading role in convincing academic institutions that their reward system is not necessarily appropriate for all academic archaeologists?

- How are we going to train scholars to research such fundamental issues as the psychology of collecting, the dynamics of the antiquities trade, and archaeological tourism?

- How are we going to expand the domain of archaeology to embrace the important lessons given us by Native American culture, oral traditions, and legend, so that all of us, professional and lay person alike, truly respect our prehistoric past?

- Above all, how do we convince people the archaeological record is important for more than just its value as a curiosity and for the tourist dollars it brings in?

There are those among you who claim that we have convinced our colleagues that public awareness is important. Maybe we have—at a superficial level. But where are the lasting curricular changes and shifts in research priorities which are a tangible reflection of a changing concern? Only a few institutions and archaeologists have begun to look a generation ahead. These issues are as important to archaeology as the discovery of the Tomb of Tutankhamen or the radiocarbon dating of maize in the Mississippi Valley, simply because the future of the past depends on how we resolve them.

The preservation of this past will not come easily. We face the seductive lures of material gain, of untold riches wrested from the artifacts of the past. We face entrenched academic values, which steer the careers of many young and talented archaeologists along sterile, already too specialized paths. In our arrogance, we also assume that everyone has a latent interest in the past. They do not, but we should at least give them respect for the lessons and perspectives that come to us from our ancestors.

And everyone should have the opportunity to enjoy and appreciate the past as we have. I remember the soft Greek spring light bathing the great amphitheater in a pink-brown light. Epidauros was quiet, the afternoon wind hushed, a faint scent of pine resin on the air. I sat high in the tiered seats, gazing down on the paved, circular stage far below. A gray-haired German Classics professor ushered a small group of elderly tourists to seats in the stalls. He stood at center stage, transformed himself into an actor of long-gone days, recited an immortal passage from Euripides' *Ion*. The ancient stanzas eddied and whirled across the vast theater, echoing high in the still air. No microphones, no amplifiers, just the brilliant acoustics of Classical times. Just for a moment, I was transported back in time to the days when Athens flowered with lustrous civilization.

Like all of you, I want my granddaughters to enjoy the delicious, provocative experience of the past. Let's do all we can to bequeath them a new archaeological world.

References Cited

Clark, J. G. D.
1937 *Archaeology and Society*. Methuen, London.

Kurten, B.
1984 *How to Deep Freeze a Mammoth*. Columbia University Press, New York.

Marquardt, W. H.
1994 "The Role of Archaeology in Raising Environmental Consciousness: An Example from Southwest Florida." In *Historical Ecology*, edited by C. Crumley, pp. 203–222. School of American Research Press, Santa Fe.

Brian Fagan teaches anthropology and archaeology at the University of California-Santa Barbara.

WORKSHOP

EDUCATION

GEORGE SMITH, chair

The Education Workshop addressed ways to increase and improve public awareness of archaeology and archaeological site protection in the Americas. Four topical work groups were created to address these critical issues—Network, Education Resource Forum and Resource Center, Formal Education, and Professional Involvement. Each work group examined ways to improve archaeological awareness and site protection by 1) coordinating archaeological education efforts through the SAA Executive Office, 2) making use of existing networks and exploring applications of the "electronic superhighway," 3) increasing multiculturalism in archaeology education programs and using archaeology to teach multiculturalism, 4) reaching a wider and more diverse audience with archaeology education, 5) expanding the international component of archaeology education programs, 6) evaluating messages and programs that relate to archaeology, and 7) coordinating archaeology education efforts with other programs.

The Network Work Group addressed ways to expand and develop a system for the exchange and dissemination of information and ideas relating to archaeology education.

The Education Resource Forum and Resource Center Work Group addressed ways to expand, develop, evaluate, and display current archaeology education materials exhibited at professional meetings and to maintain a listing of such materials to be disseminated to various individuals, groups, organizations, and institutions. In addition, this work group considered the establishment of an Education Resource Center to conduct and coordinate research, program development, and training.

The Formal Education Work Group examined ways to strengthen the quality and quantity of precollegiate archaeology education resources available to students, educators, and professional archaeologists by evaluating materials and encouraging closer communication and collaboration between educators and archaeologists.

The Professional Involvement Work Group discussed ways to increase education, training, and involvement of professional archaeologists in a wide variety of archaeology education activities.

Background on the Education Workshop

The Education Workshop was based on work begun by the SAA Public Education Committee (PEC), a committee formally established in April 1990 by the SAA Executive Board. The committee traces its beginnings to an ad hoc work group formed during the first Save the Past for the Future conference held in Taos, New Mexico, in 1989. A follow-up meeting in Minneapolis in 1989 as part of the Presenting the Past to the Public conference series led to the establishment of a Task Force on Public Education and the development of an action plan in 1990. The action plan became a strategic plan in 1992. Both the Taos and Breckenridge workshops owe their beginnings to SAA's Save the Past for the Future project initiated in 1988 and kicked off in a special session at the 1989 SAA meetings in Atlanta entitled Our Vanishing Past.

The direction provided by the PEC over the past five years formed the basis for the topics selected for the 1994 Education Workshop. These topics were directed at promoting archaeology public education to increase understanding and appreciation for the past with the goal of encouraging greater preservation and protection of cultural resources in the Americas. More specifically, the basic premise of the Education Workshop and the PEC was, and is, that sharing archaeology with the public provides a sense of who we are as human beings; promotes cultural awareness and sensitivity; provides a means of teaching critical thinking, cooperative learning, problem solving, and citizenship skills; increases awareness of archaeological research; and promotes stewardship of archaeological resources.

Participants

In any creative endeavor, success is directly related to the individuals who participate and their ability to function as a team. Selection of the Education Workshop team was an arduous task. From a list of more than 150 highly qualified individuals, 70 were invited to participate. Criteria for selection were based on team building around the four work group topics. An effort was made to provide continuity by having representatives who had attended the Taos conference also participate in the Breckenridge conference. As a result, each work group contained one or more people who had attended the Taos meeting. To provide diversity in topic discussion, representatives from federal and state government, academic institutions, the private sector, museums, Native American groups, and other professional organizations in the United States, Canada, and Latin America, were invited. Due in most part to the lack of travel funds to attend the conference, Latin American representation was limited. Future public education efforts should strive to facilitate increased representation from Latin American countries. In addition, geographical and gender representation was sought as well as representation from the PEC. Fifty-one highly motivated archaeologists, museum personnel, and educators ultimately participated in the Education Workshop.

The Education Workshop was chaired by George Smith, Ed Friedman, and Kevin Kilcullen. The four work groups were

Network—Beverly Mitchum and Teresa Hoffman, chairs; Jim Bruseth, Joelle Clark, Susan Collins, Ann Early, Michael Graves, Dan Haas, Gwynn Henderson, Dorothy Krass, and Anne Pyburn

Education Resource Forum/ Resource Center—KC Smith and Nancy Hawkins, chairs; J. Barto Arnold, Bob Brunswig, Amy Douglass, Megg Heath, Meggett Lavin, Phyllis Messenger, and Judy Proper

Formal Education—Shelley Smith, Richard Brook, and Karolyn Smardz, chairs; Elizabeth Baquedano, Bill Butler, Daphne Derven, Carol Ellick, Virginia Horak, Cathy MacDonald, Jeanne Moe, Connie Nobles, Pam Wheat, Nancy White, Joyce Williams, Martha Williams, and Sandra Zacharias

Professional Involvement—Susan

Bender and Shereen Lerner, chairs; Judy Bense, Hester Davis, Jim Dixon, Patrick Garrow, Mark Lynott, Frank McManamon, David Pokotylo, Ruth Selig, Dean Snow, and Renata Wolynec

Work group chairs gave freely of their time and expertise to organize, implement, and compile the results of the workshop. Through their dedication, experience, and personal involvement in public education, and their ability to focus the tremendous energy exhibited by work group members, they exceeded expectations.

The depth and quality of discussions addressing the four work group topics and the well-conceived recommendations are directly attributable to the individual work group members. Their diverse backgrounds, talents, and ability to function as part of a team provided depth of coverage to each of the topics.

The following recommendations compiled by the workshop are designed to increase and improve public understanding of and appreciation for the past and archaeological resource protection in the Americas.

Network Work Group

This group was an outgrowth of the PEC Network Subcommittee. As teachers and other interested members of the public contacted the PEC and began to receive its newsletter, it became clear that a list of archaeologists and educators was needed who would function as local contacts/coordinators for SAA archaeology education programs and resources. Currently the Network Subcommittee has identified coordinators for most states and Canadian provinces. These coordinators serve as "gatekeepers" to gather and disseminate information among national, state, and local archaeologists, educators, and consumers. However, given the magnitude of such a network, it was critical that issues of structure, responsibilities, and support be addressed.

To this end, the Network Work Group developed guidelines for defining the function of a network coordinator, considered resources to assist coordinators, and established ways to evaluate the effectiveness of both the network and the coordinators. A functional statement was developed describing some of the resources that would be helpful to coordinators and responsibilities they might undertake. Guidelines for developing a sourcebook for coordinators and methods to evaluate and improve the effectiveness of coordinators were defined.

The functional statement identified aspects of the position that should be considered prior to accepting a volunteer network coordinator position. These include availability of institutional support (not required but helpful), membership in SAA, familiarity with the local archaeological community, and a willingness to undertake the position for at least two years. Responsibilities would include compiling lists of archaeologists willing to serve as resource people for teachers; following up on contacts with teachers who initially contact the PEC and providing resource materials; working with education and social science departments and providing assistance and materials; displaying PEC products at archaeological, educational, and other appropriate meetings and conferences; putting teachers in touch with other teachers; and using electronic networks to communicate with teachers and schools about archaeology education programs and products.

The sourcebook would contain information and ideas to help coordinators with their assignments. It also would include examples of successful programs from other locations, ideas for establishing contacts with different constituencies, and ways to identify local resources.

Evaluation of coordinators would be undertaken through a reporting system in which each coordinator annually summarized his or her activities.

Also addressed were ways to expand the network to reach additional constituencies, especially private landowners who control archaeological sites on their property. Emphasis was placed on ways to reach and educate landowners. It was recommended that a subcommittee of the PEC focusing on landowner education issues be established. A second recommendation was to develop state-specific information about programs and assistance for landowners interested in site preservation and to prepare a booklet advocating site preservation targeted to private landowners. In addition, a recommendation was made to create an inventory of existing communication networks already reaching private landowners, and to monitor and disseminate information on proposed and existing legislation that involves private property.

Expanding the network communication system by promoting the use of computerized networks also was addressed. The use of computerized networks as the primary means of developing and expanding current information and resource networks with special emphasis on enhancing communication among diverse groups was considered. It was recommended that a computerized network system situated in the SAA executive office be developed. Coordination of the system would be one of the responsibilities undertaken by a new SAA position, education coordinator, a position endorsed by all four work groups. This would be an important step in SAA's effort to strengthen ties and information exchange throughout the Americas.

Given the need to secure both human and financial resources for the network, it was recommended that a development director be hired to identify and develop funding sources for public education programs.

Education Resource Forum and Resource Center Work Group

The task before the Education Resource Forum/Resource Center Work Group was to assess the PEC sponsored traveling exhibit of precollegiate archaeology education materials and its accompanying bibliographic guide. The members also considered and proposed criteria for developing one or more SAA-sponsored or supported resource centers offering a variety of services including in-house libraries, research, and training programs. Both topics reflect SAA's commitment to improving and increasing public access to archaeology-related information and activities.

The Education Resource Forum is an outgrowth of an action item included in the PEC's strategic plan. While the action item originally called for a "marketplace" for educational products, the format that subsequently evolved consisted of a traveling display of teaching materials for precollegiate audiences that could be sent to local, regional, and national conferences across the nation. Initially presented as books, manuals, games, and other publications laid humbly on tables, with only a hint of descriptive signage, the traveling exhibit received a complete facelift in 1993 with the addition of furniture to enhance presentation and effectiveness. However, with the addition of more professional-looking elements came substantial weight and bulk, rendering the exhibit more difficult and more costly to send to conferences, particularly smaller venues. Moreover, in the short time since the exhibit's makeover, the quantity of resource materials available for display literally has outgrown the exhibit space, and the need for selective criteria, based on quality control as well as space factors, has become apparent.

Work group members endorsed the strategy of disseminating information about teaching resources as a means of engendering and facilitating the incorporation of precollegiate archaeology education into a variety of settings. They agreed that a more portable and efficient traveling exhibit is needed—one that consolidates and refines resource information, incorporates electronic learning devices, and presents additional messages about the purpose of the Education Resource Forum and the objectives of SAA. Several strategies to reach these goals were discussed. Foremost was the designation of a task force to analyze and recommend alternatives for fabrication of a new exhibit. As a means of reducing the volume of display items, the preparation of notebooks with area-specific (i.e., by country, region, state, etc.) information about educational materials and programs was recommended in lieu of actually displaying items. It further was recommended that the development of criteria to evaluate materials placed in these notebooks or on exhibit shelves be updated to ensure that messages inappropriate to archaeology education or SAA are not included. To facilitate the use of resource materials by educators, annotation of the bibliographic guide that accompanies the exhibit and electronic dissemination of the guide were recommended. However, recognizing that the development of such alternative strategies will take time for fund raising and fabrication, the work group proposed that the current Education Resource Forum continue to be used for two more years, as long as a few structural modifications can be made to the exhibit, and with the understanding that efforts to initiate the use of area-specific resource notebooks will begin.

In addition to continuing use of the existing exhibit, the work group recommended that a task force be established to study, analyze, and make recommendations about the design and fabrication of a new Education Resource Forum, and that a set of criteria be developed for evaluating materials included in the forum to assure their appropriateness and to determine the best means of entering the evaluated and annotated resource guide into an electronic information system for direct access by teachers, educators, and archaeologists. To assist with information dissemination, the development of a brochure describing the objectives, activities, and products of the Public Education Committee also was recommended.

The concept of a Resource Center was formalized with the revised PEC strategic plan of 1992. An action item was proposed encouraging the development of facilities at institutions of higher learning and/or federal agency regional centers to provide a variety of services and activities relating to archaeology and education.

The work group acknowledged that if archaeology and cultural resource education are to have any long-term impact, educational resource centers must be established to conduct and coordinate research and program development. In addition to being think tanks for educators and archaeologists, such facilities could provide training, internship, conference, and research opportunities, and serve as repositories and clearinghouses for resource materials and information relating to archaeology education. The work group considered a variety of organizational arrangements—from the development of a single centrally located office to regional centers allied with governmental or private institutions—looking at a number of existing facilities as possible models or sites. Members agreed that a prototypic center, focusing on precollegiate archaeology education issues, would be most appropriate, expanding later in number of centers and range of audience. They also suggested that, while all facilities should have certain common policies and services, each center might develop specialized program areas. Based on this premise, it was recommended that a task force be established to study and examine various strategies to coordinate the Resource Center and other partnerships with existing institutions for public education programs.

Formal Education Work Group

This work group began by noting that the archaeological profession and related professions have made great strides in advancing the stewardship message through archaeology education programs. Numerous programs focused on school-aged children are offered formally in schools and also in less formal settings such as museums, nature centers, and youth groups. Over the past five years, the PEC has sponsored many events, including workshops and symposia, and prepared materials on archaeology education, resulting in a closer alliance between archaeologists and educators. Some archaeologists have observed a reduction in looting and vandalism in their area, which they attribute to archaeology education.

These accomplishments are notable and due in part to PEC's initiative. A strong foundation has been laid and a wide network built. The Formal Education Work Group agreed that it is time to address the goal of strengthening the quality and quantity of precollegiate archaeology education resources and programs. After listing several dozen ideas about how to meet the goal, items were grouped into categories. The work group then identified various strategies and made recommendations for each.

The work group felt it was necessary to assess existing materials and determine which ones best meet the needs of educators and students and also promote stewardship of cultural resources. The archaeological message and pedagogical elements need to be examined, with the guidelines under development by the PEC Formal Education Committee as a beginning point. Recommendations for achieving this included conducting both an evaluation of the current level of the K–12 students' and teachers' archaeological knowledge, and a longitudinal study of the effectiveness of educational programs to instill an ethic of stewardship in students. Examples and descriptions of evaluation processes then could be provided to developers of new materials.

The Formal Education Work Group concluded that for an archaeology program to be effective and used by teachers, it is important that education programs use the most appropriate and current educational materials. Mechanisms recommended to facilitate this included

- Forming alliances with educators and involving them in curricula review, development, and implementation
- Developing feedback loops between educators and archaeologists developing programs
- Preparing and updating an annotated bibliography of current educational methodologies and trends

Another observation made by the

work group was that by and large, when archaeology is taught in the classroom, it is at the initiative and interest of a teacher who finds a way to include it in a crowded curriculum. To enlist the widest participation from teachers, archaeology must "officially" be incorporated into standard school curricula. Tactics to accomplish this goal could take place on the national, state/provincial, and local levels, requiring archaeologists to be involved as standards are developed and updated. In addition, archaeologists will need to form cooperative liaisons with teacher associations and administrators.

Also identified by the work group was that a critical link in widely establishing archaeology education programs is to get appropriate resources to the people who need them. The target groups here are educators and professionals in cultural heritage fields who are practicing public archaeology. While the audiences and types of information differ, some of the communication links can work for both groups. Recommendations included

• Establishing a clearinghouse for disseminating information and materials and securing coordinators for Canada, the United States, and Latin America

• Sponsoring a Western Hemisphere meeting to develop the network and identify institutional participants

• Establishing regional resource centers in the Americas

Other mechanisms could be expanded, such as the PEC newsletter, the Resource Forum, Internet, and satellite downloading of video media. Translation services will be necessary to share information widely.

The work group felt that it was timely and appropriate that anthropology address current societal problems and issues; archaeology education can be a basis from which to encourage inter- and intracultural respect and understanding. Archaeology can substantially contribute to understanding both cultural diversity and the commonality of the human experience, and can help teachers teach about multicultural issues. Recommendations to achieve this included producing videos and printed materials for classroom use and translating them into appropriate languages; actively seeking representation from culturally diverse educators and archaeologists; developing guidelines; and establishing an education coordinator position in the SAA's executive office.

Recommendations made as part of this work group outlined a comprehensive and practical approach to expanding the quality and quantity of archaeology education and the stewardship message into the next century across the Americas.

Professional Involvement Work Group

This work group identified professional archaeologists as an integral component in assuring the long-term success of public education activities, whether these are aimed at the general public or students in formal classroom settings at all educational levels.

In an ideal world, professional résumés would routinely include evidence of public education work, while archaeology curricula would reinforce the value of public education. At the graduate level, a public archaeology course would become a consistent feature of degree requirements, and undergraduate courses would include public archaeology issues and training as a recurrent theme. Sustained public education activity among archaeologists also would be used to address multicultural issues, helping to build strong ties with Native American communities.

Finally, archaeology education

activities would become the vehicle for creating partnerships with disciplines having allied interests, such as museum studies and public history. In short, the ideal world would be one in which public education would be a valued and accepted component of archaeologists' professional lives, and adherence to this standard would promote public awareness of numerous issues vital to the discipline, including cultural resource preservation, continued public and governmental support for archaeology, and validation (through public outreach projects) of post-secondary archaeology curricula.

We are, however, still far from this ideal world.

Many professional archaeologists do not participate in public education because it seems at odds with their career aspirations. That is, time spent in public education is time not spent on those activities more routinely recognized by the profession as measures of professional success. In addition, many graduate and undergraduate programs do not provide students with adequate training in public archaeology. This is important because priorities for professional careers are set in place and validated during graduate training.

The Professional Involvement Work Group was convened to identify initiatives that might serve to increase the education, training, and involvement of professional archaeologists in a wide variety of archaeology education activities. Recommendations are intended to promote professional involvement by providing incentives for undertaking public education work, training in how to undertake such work successfully, and education about the range of opportunities available in public education.

Members of the work group recommended that steps be taken to formally recognize public education activities as a significant professional activity. SAA initiatives to validate public education should include

- establishing a public education coordinator in the SAA executive office with responsibility for promoting and supporting public education activities across the discipline
- making the PEC newsletter a benefit of SAA membership
- surveying academic departments about their current levels of engagement and reward structure for public education activity
- establishing a comprehensive and meaningful award structure that recognizes excellence in public education, with at least one of these awards recognizing outstanding graduate student work
- identifying and encouraging publication outlets for public education activity

Articles on the "method and theory" of public education should have a place in our professional literature if we intend to recognize this work as critical scholarly activity. Similarly, reviews of popular books, museum exhibits, and videos have a place in this literature. Developing a popular publication series should be considered. A letter should be written to college and university administrators, which explains that disciplinary standards include public education as a significant scholarly activity. From this perspective, writing for the public is, for example, as important as writing for professional peers. In addition, SAA should work together with government agencies to draft a plan for requiring public education and outreach activities for publicly funded or permitted archaeological projects.

The work group concluded that while many archaeologists may have a general sympathy for the value of public education, they are not likely to have specific training in those skills necessary for public outreach. SAA needs to provide professional development opportunities for its membership and the regular inclusion of such training in graduate curricula. It will be far easier to implement an ethic of public education once professionals have the vision and skills that flow from adequate training.

In order to achieve this goal, the work group recommended that workshops on various aspects of public education activity be offered routinely at professional meetings. SAA's membership should be surveyed to determine those workshop topics likely to be of greatest interest and impact. Steps need to be taken to encourage the inclusion of an applied curriculum at the graduate and undergraduate levels. Sample syllabi and examples of internship or directed study projects should be compiled for distribution to departments of anthropology. A sample curriculum should be prepared for those departments interested in offering a professional master's degree. Departments of anthropology offering field opportunities should be encouraged to include a public education component in these experiences. This activity might include giving tours, preparing brochures or temporary exhibits, working with volunteers, or developing source material for teaching public archaeology.

Because many archaeologists may not be aware of the range of opportunities that are available to support public education as an important component in professional development, dissemination of such information will encourage wider participation in a variety of public education activities. To achieve this it is recommended that SAA maintain a list of granting opportunities in public education for all members. The list should be available both electronically (Internet, for example) and in published format in the PEC newsletter. A list, which could be distributed electronically, also should be maintained of employment opportunities in public education. Regional professional organizations should be encouraged to establish a speakers bureau. A subset of professionals listed in the bureau would be available to graduate and undergraduate departments to present information on model public education programs.

The work group identified a set of core issues that crosscut all of their recommendations, as well as those of several other work groups. These can serve as a framework for all public education efforts. First, public education will be most effective if it is based on an accurate understanding of public attitudes about archaeology. Hence, it was recommended that a professional organization be contacted to conduct a national survey aimed at providing the SAA membership with the information requisite for drafting and targeting appropriate messages about archaeology. Second, public education should also be used to build stronger ties to those groups with which archaeologists have overlapping concerns and interests, specifically the indigenous peoples of the Americas and the avocational archaeologists who share an interest in reconstructing and protecting the past. A series of specific steps should be taken to strengthen these ties through organizational structure and the identification of the educational interests and needs of these groups. Third, exchange should be fostered with other professional societies that undertake public education about the past. This effort would enable membership to stay current with developments in related fields, while helping to ensure a more holistic approach to the preservation and conservation of all cultural resources.

Conclusion

During the Education Workshop, the individual work groups suggested numerous ways in which SAA can increase public education and archaeological site protection. Some can be undertaken immediately with minimal funding; others will require additional planning and funding. All, however, are achievable. Of critical importance is the establishment of the education coordinator position in the SAA executive office. This position is key to the ongoing success of the society's education and site protection efforts and will function as a key component in all future archaeology and education plans. Increasing undergraduate and graduate training in public archaeology will greatly increase the society's long-term efforts to protect the past and present the past to the public. Establishment of resource center(s), which would act as a focal point for materials, training, internships, networks, and programs, would greatly facilitate public outreach as it pertains to archaeology. If we are to understand public attitudes regarding archaeology and encourage stewardship, it is imperative that surveys be developed, undertaken, and the results analyzed in an effort to develop effective programs that will make the most efficient use of limited human and financial resources. If the recommendations resulting from the working conference are to be achieved, it is necessary to begin work immediately. Task forces should be formed and funding plans developed for the recommendations that were made.

In addition to the conference report, the workshop chairs will also prepare a detailed action plan. This plan will include specific information on each of the recommendations made including discussion, time frame, estimated cost, sources of funding, participation, and coordination. This will form the basis for implementing recommendations.

If we are to save the past for the future, it is imperative that we not only be good learners but good communicators as well. If a major goal of a university education is to involve students in the scholarly process, we might do well to consider Chaucer's observation that learning and teaching are part of a single system. We also might attend to his understanding that the scholarly way of life is a pleasure-driven system. Its participants communicate enthusiasm and enjoyment as well as knowledge.

WORKSHOP

INTEGRATED RESOURCE MANAGEMENT

MARILYN NICKELS, chair

The Integrated Resource Management Workshop, also known as the Human Dimensions of Ecosystem Management Workshop, focused on the role of archaeological resources and archaeology as a discipline in the implementation of ecosystem management. Ecosystem management is an approach to the management of natural resources that attempts to use an understanding of natural systems and processes in order to realize optimum conditions for ensuring long-term ecological sustainability. The workshop members discussed the many contributions archaeological resources can make to this understanding.

It should be acknowledged from the outset that this topic was included in the Breckenridge conference agenda only after some lengthy discussion. Even at the conference itself, some participants raised serious questions about the rationale for including this topic in a conference on the protection of archaeological sites. Workshop attendees responded to this concern by pointing out that archaeological sites will only be protected so long as the public (including landowners and land managers) understand the unique contribution of archaeological resources and knowledge to contemporary life. This workshop established as its mission, therefore, recommendations to improve the management and protection of cultural and natural resources by providing unique insight into the long-term interaction of human communities with the environment. In the words of the preamble of the National Historic Preservation Act: "...the historical and cultural foundations of the Nation should be preserved as a living part of our community life and development in order to give a sense of orientation to the American people."

Since this topic was new to an SAA-sponsored conference, the attendees represented a wide range of professionals from government agencies, universities, and consulting firms. In addition, although most individuals were archaeologists and/or cultural resource specialists, some biologists and representatives of other disciplines also participated. The workshop began, therefore, with a series of broad exploratory discussions, which are presented more fully below under "Preliminary Discussion." These discussions included 1) the development of a policy statement on the role of archaeology in ecosystem management, 2) factors in the current management of archaeological resources that do or do not contribute toward this more integrated approach, 3) models and methodologies for regional alignments in integrated resource management, 4) the use of traditional cultural knowledge as a resource in ecosystem management, and 5) the possible ingredients for a handbook or other practical tool for carrying out integrated resource management.

After much discussion, certain

conclusions emerged. All participants agreed that, while ecosystem management is a tool being supported heavily as an approach to the management of public land, it has application to the management of all landscapes. Indeed, one of the hallmarks of this approach is to de-emphasize artificial administrative boundaries that have little meaning in the understanding of ecological processes. Therefore, an integrated resource management approach has potential implications for encouraging the protection and use of information from cultural resources on private as well as public land. In addition, all participants agreed that ecosystem management is a method that emphasizes biological resources, but it will have little success unless archaeologists and other scholars in the cultural disciplines bring to the table an awareness of human beings as a biological resource who have had and continue to have a profound impact on the landscape. Finally, the participants emphasized that contemporary natural landscapes must be viewed on a continuum in time, with an understanding that the discipline of archaeology, with its sister disciplines of history, anthropology, geography and other sciences, have an enormous amount of data and understanding to offer to our knowledge of the evolution of particular landscapes, including the rate and sources of change. This contribution is accompanied by a dependence of archaeology and other cultural disciplines on several natural sciences for a wide range of methodologies and data. It only make sense, therefore, to manage resources by integrating the work of all relevant disciplines with one another.

The first two days of the workshop, as mentioned above, broke the topic into several elements, which were addressed in small discussion groups and the conclusions shared at the end of each session. These subtopics were designed merely to stimulate ideas and, remarkably, led the group to create new approaches to the subject matter throughout the week. Out of this dialogue grew the rationale for the specific action items that workshop participants agreed to implement in the months and years ahead.

Preliminary Discussion

The preliminary discussion was divided into the following major questions.

1. What is the role of cultural disciplines in ecosystem management?

During this wide-ranging discussion, most participants lamented the fact that ecosystem management is a biological/ecological term that views human beings more often than not as an intrusion on the landscape, rather than as another biological resource. In addition, the term frequently is used to mean the management of a contemporary landscape with little or no consideration of any time dimension. Thus disciplines such as archaeology and history appear to have no contribution to make to the field. Some participants resisted the notion of merely "contributing" within a biologically dominated framework, but many also acknowledged that the framework has already been developed, especially in federal agencies, and therefore it cannot be ignored. In considering the contribution of cultural disciplines, many participants underlined the environmental data collected by archaeologists, the data on human occupation, use and manipulation of a landscape, and the critical analysis of cultural adaptation and cultural differences composing so much of the work of archaeologists. Indeed, some participants pointed out that certain cultural constructs govern the development of an approach like ecosystem management itself. There were many suggestions for the development of a position paper on the role of cultural disciplines in ecosystem management, with a call for collaboration with related disciplines, such as history and anthropology, in this effort. Finally, many participants had examples of specific projects in which they had been involved in which archaeological and historical data had contributed to the understanding and management of a natural landscape.

2. How do we make the transition from the old cultural resource management approach to an ecosystem management one?

Much of this discussion centered around the domination in the field of cultural resource management of cultural compliance activities, that is, compliance with Section 106 of the National Historic Preservation Act, which consists of clearing projects on public and private land by considering the impact of a proposed activity, project by project, site by site, on significant cultural resources. Almost all participants agreed that unless government agencies and, therefore, those who work with or for them, move to a broader approach to the management of archaeological resources, little contribution could be made to ecosystem management. Several individuals also made the point that the failure to synthesize the data resulting from this compliance archaeology has left the field with little ability to easily share knowledge that might inform ecosystem management decision making. The group generally concluded that land management agencies need to find a way to emphasize Section 110 of the National Historic Preservation Act, which calls for broad inventory and assessment of the resource base itself, if a true contribution to ecosystem management is to occur. In some real way, however, the ecosystem management approach, with an emphasis on larger geographic landscapes, regardless of ownership or management patterns, provides a unique opportunity to move to a broader framework for inventory and analysis of cultural resources.

3. How do archaeologists integrate cultural landscapes with the geographic scales that make sense in an ecosystem management approach?

This discussion, while fruitful, did not lead to many concrete conclusions. Many participants acknowledged that few archaeologists and other cultural specialists compare questions of scale in their own disciplines with those of biologists or ecologists, or vice versa. Probably the most important fact was simply that greater dialogue is needed on this issue. Some individuals were concerned that research questions often must define scale, but research-based definitions are often different from those that suit immediate management needs. Scale and boundaries will also vary on the same landscape even among cultural specialists, depending on the time period and other factors brought to bear in viewing a particular location. Finally, just as the disciplines of biology and ecology are looking at fluid definitions of boundary and scale, so must the cultural disciplines see this issue as one that is evolving rather than static.

4. What role can traditional cultural knowledge play in ecosystem management?

While this term has been used most often in recent years to refer to contributions of Native American cultural traditions to the study and management of cultural and natural resources, most participants were concerned to use the broadest possible definition of this knowledge; that is, generations of knowledge specific to a community, whatever the community may be. This knowledge ranges from specific information on the biological resource in a given area to belief systems regarding landscapes or sites to customs and practices that have a bearing on our knowledge of an ecosystem. Since this information is usually held within a community and has not been the subject of scientific scrutiny in the usual sense, there is often prejudice regarding its utility. At the same time, the community may have a variety of reasons, from religious beliefs to genuine skepticism, for being reluctant to share the knowledge. At the same time, archaeologists and anthropologists often have training that makes them an obvious source of technical capability in obtaining traditional cultural knowledge from those who are willing to share it. In addition, the participation of a local community in a project is essential for the complete success of ecosystem management efforts. Finally, many communities may have genuine insights into the ecosystem management approach itself, thus making dialogue a worthwhile endeavor.

5. What practical guidance would be worth developing to enhance the role of the cultural disciplines in ecosystem management?

This discussion began with a suggestion for a handbook of practical guidance on how to incorporate archaeological and historical information into ecosystem management. The workshop discussion on this subject centered on a definition of the audience for such a handbook and, based on the audience, some possible topics. Most participants agreed that no single written product would serve the many audiences which need to be reached. Instead, some suggested that workshop participants and others be willing to contact organizations and agencies for opportunities to "spread the word," including articles in newsletters, sessions at professional meetings of biologists and ecologists, and opportunities to meet with or address managers of federal agencies and other institutions. Some also suggested that academic institutions needed to be encouraged to revise the curriculum in archaeology in order to incorporate a more interdisciplinary approach in graduate programs. Indeed, students in a wide variety of disciplines need to be encouraged to see collaborative efforts as the future course in most professions. Finally, the advent of telecommunications capability, such as Internet and other tools, makes it possible to share practical guidance in this area very easily across geographic, organizational and disciplinary lines.

Action Items

The workshop concentrated on several major action items flowing from the discussion. The emphasis, in fact, throughout the conference was on changing the way archaeologists and other scientists do business in the real world of resource management. The following action items were adopted as a beginning point for such change.

- Develop a policy statement that outlines the role of archaeology and archaeological resources in managing landscapes in a more ecologically sensitive manner. Pat Barker of the Bureau of Land Management agreed to head a small committee to begin this process. Other groups committed themselves to assist in the distribution of this statement to a wide range of audiences.

- Begin collecting examples of integrated resource management already in practice and produce an annotated listing and bibliography of these examples. Prepare a poster for the 1995 SAA meeting using some of these examples.

Investigate publishing the best and most instructive examples as a monograph for wider distribution within the archaeological community, other disciplines, land management agencies and environmental organizations. Andrew Yatsko of the U.S. Navy agreed to begin this process.

• Develop an outreach plan to contact other organizations and agencies to express the interest of archaeologists in integrated resource management approaches. This would include assembling and disseminating an annotated directory of journals and other publications on ecosystem management-related topics to which archaeologists could submit articles, as well as an annotated directory of governmental agencies and nongovernmental organizations involved in research and application of ecosystem management, which would be receptive to hearing from archaeologists interested in closer collaboration at conferences and meetings. Produce public service announcements on the contributions of cultural disciplines to ecosystem management. Lobby with various offices and committees on Capitol Hill, as well as with other branches of government at the federal, state and local levels, to make clear the importance of cultural disciplines to the effectiveness of ecosystem management. Al Tonetti of the Ohio Historical Society will head a group of participants who volunteered to work on this effort.

• Transform the cultural resource management function encompassed largely within the framework of compliance with Section 106 of the National Historic Preservation Act, so that it becomes more fully directed toward effective integrated resource management. Arrange to make a presentation at the next meeting of the National Conference of State Historic Preservation Officers in order to request participation in an effort to transform the process of compliance with Section 106 into a more effective tool for preserving archaeological resources as sources of information on past environmental conditions and impacts. Re-orient the work of federal agencies so that implementation of Section 110 of the NHPA, for inventory and management of cultural resources, is emphasized as a mechanism for capturing the research value of archaeological sites and, more importantly, patterns of sites, in revealing the actual status of past landscapes, as well as the pattern of land uses over time leading to the appearance of the present landscape. Mike Kaczor of the Soil Conservation Service is heading a committee to move these actions forward.

• Create and support a technology subcommittee on information resources management for SAA. (This proposal has been merged with the work of the SAA committee on technology.) Provide a technology seminar at SAA's annual meeting. Take an active role in promoting the use of GIS, GPS, and related technologies among archaeologists, in order to enhance communication capability and data sharing with other scientific disciplines. Establish a hub for SAA on World-Wide Web, so that interactive capability and networking can occur on integrated resource management and across disciplines, geographic distances, and other constricting factors, leading to much more effective ecosystem management. Marcy Gray of Gray and Associates offered to move these action items forward with a small group of volunteers.

• Establish a new SAA committee to deal specifically with ecosystem management, giving it the ability to move forward the agenda of the workshop. This committee could encompass many of the action items above, such as outreach, technology, training, and transforming cultural resource management practice. It would also concentrate its efforts on fostering undergraduate and graduate courses as well as postgraduate training in ecosystem management as it affects archaeological research and cultural preservation. Cal Jennings of Colorado State University agreed to serve as the head of this group.

Conclusion

The Integrated Resource Management Workshop was a beginning. Its recommendations should be viewed as part of the larger conference framework, and thus related to those of the other two workshops. Finally, perhaps the major outcome of this effort was the realization that, for many reasons, integrated resource management represents a true effort to save the archaeological past in order to build a reliable future. The greatest challenge of the late twentieth and early twenty-first century is to ensure the prosperity of global populations in an ecologically sustainable environment. What could be more important in meeting that challenge than understanding past communities and environments that have shaped the world in which we live?

WORKSHOP

LAW ENFORCEMENT

ROBERT MARRIOTT, chair

The 45 participants in the Law Enforcement Workshop considered five topics related to protecting archaeological sites from looting and vandalism. These topics were prosecution and legislation; training; interagency cooperation; information sharing; and investigative technologies.

Five task groups were formed to consider these topics:

Prosecution and Legislation—Michael Boynton, Clay Davis, Pat Lyng, Larry Mackey, Dennis McLane, Judy Reed, Lynell Schalk, Robert Simmons, Rick Thornton

Training—Tony Bonanno, Dan Fromstein, Allen Funkhouser, Cecil Ison, Maggie Johnston, Woody Jones, Martin McAllister

Interagency Cooperation—Randy Bramer, Jonathan Dover, Bob Gough, Cheryl Munson, Jim Rogers, Rigby Wright, Phil Young

Information Sharing—Tom Des Jean, Rick Dougherty, Tom Lister, Art Lunkley, Anne Rogers, David Tarler

Investigative Technologies—Paul Berkowitz, Pete Deane, John Diefenbach, Jeff Kent, Susan Morton, Jim Moriarty, Martin Phillips, Erv Taylor

The task groups developed 58 recommendations on the five topics considered, all arranged here in priority order under their task group headings. Twenty-nine were recommendations for short- and long-term actions by the Society for American Archaeology (SAA). The other 29 were recommendations for short- and long-term actions by agencies.

Prosecution and Legislation

The goal of the Prosecution and Legislation Task Group (Judy Reed, chair, Rick Thornton, recorder) was to identify what can be done to obtain more successful prosecutions under federal cultural resource and property laws. This group developed 11 recommendations (1–8, short term; 9–11, long term). Three of these recommendations are measures recommended at the 1989 Save the Past for the Future conference, which have yet to be acted on or which require additional action. Each carry-over recommendation is identified as a "1989 recommendation" in the listing that follows:

- SAA should propose to the U.S. Sentencing Commission that they adopt specific guidelines for ARPA sentencing.
- SAA should sponsor the adoption of guidelines for ARPA site damage assessments, including sources for commercial value appraisals.
- DOJ should transfer ARPA and Native American Graves Protection and Repatriation Act (NAGPRA) prosecutions to their Lands and Resources Section where other resources cases are currently handled.
- SAA should create an ARPA reward program (1989 recommendation).
- Federal agencies should have

staff specialists who are experts in ARPA prosecutions and should develop an "incident command system" to utilize these specialists on an interagency basis.

- Federal agencies should make increased use of the civil penalty provisions of ARPA in cases where criminal prosecution is declined or not appropriate.
- Federal agencies should work with U.S. attorney offices to develop prosecution guidelines where agencies have experienced difficulties in having ARPA cases accepted for prosecution.
- Federal agencies should follow DOJ standard operating procedures for responding to media inquiries regarding pending cultural resource cases and promote public awareness via press releases to the media under agency procedures after case adjudication (1989 recommendation).
- SAA should propose an amendment to ARPA that would return fines and forfeited funds to the affected agency for its own use, including payment of ARPA rewards (1989 recommendation).
- SAA should propose an amendment to NAGPRA to make the act's only threshold consistent with that of ARPA.
- Federal agencies should consider funding special prosecutors for ARPA cases.

Training

The goals of the Training Task Group (Tony Bonanno, chair, Martin McAllister, recorder) were to evaluate the appropriateness and effectiveness of existing archaeological resource protection training programs, to determine how these programs can be made more effective, and identify new types of training programs or resources needed. This group formulated 19 recommendations. Five of these recommendations are measures recommended at the 1989 Save the Past for the Future conference, which have yet to be acted on or which require additional action. Each carry-over recommendation is identified as a "1989 recommendation" in the listing that follows:

- Federal agency representatives should encourage the Federal Law Enforcement Training Center (FLETC) to continue the current block of archaeological resource protection training in the basic program because this training is appropriate and effective.
- Federal agency representatives should encourage FLETC to use archaeological resource protection examples in the basic program whenever possible (e.g., crime scene investigation, practical exercises, testifying).
- Federal agency representatives should ensure that archaeological resource protection training is part of all Law Enforcement for Land Managers programs taught at FLETC (1989 recommendation).
- SAA should encourage federal agencies to present archaeological resource protection training to agency managers at management team meetings (1989 recommendation).
- Federal agency representatives should encourage FLETC to continue the current 40-hour archaeological resource protection training program because this training is appropriate and effective (1989 recommendation).
- Federal agency representatives should encourage FLETC to increase emphasis on civil and administrative remedies in the legal block of instruction in the 40-hour archaeological resource protection training program (1989 recommendation).
- Federal agency representatives should more critically evaluate priorities for selection of participants in the 40-hour

archaeological resource protection training program based on appropriateness of the training location to the employee; regional networking opportunities; and pertinence of the training location to the employee.

• FLETC and federal agency representatives should encourage expanded participation in the 40-hour archaeological resource protection training program by other federal agencies (e.g., Federal Bureau of Investigation, U.S. Customs, National Oceanographic and Atmospheric Administration, Internal Revenue Service, Border Patrol) and by tribal, state, and local agencies.

• The NPS Archeological Assistance Division should discontinue the overview of archaeological resource protection for managers training program because this training does not appear to be effective for the target audience. The subject matter should be incorporated in agency land manager training.

• The NPS Washington office and DOJ should be encouraged to continue the archaeological resource protection training program for assistant U.S. attorneys because this training is appropriate and effective (1989 recommendation). The program should be taught at least twice a year at varying geographic locations with appropriate field sites.

• The NPS Washington office and DOJ should transfer sponsorship of the archaeological resource protection training program for assistant U.S. attorneys to the NPS office at FLETC.

• The NPS Washington office and DOJ should continue to produce, and update annually, the DOJ ARPA sourcebook and ensure distribution of the sourcebook to appropriate locations.

• Federal agency representatives and FLETC should develop an advanced archaeological resource protection training program, which would include training on undercover operations, trafficking, warrants, technical investigative equipment, site damage assessment, and other relevant topics.

• SAA should develop a site damage assessment training program for its membership.

• Federal agency representatives and FLETC should develop archaeological resource protection materials for use in regional and local training.

• Federal agency managers should make FLETC 40-hour program graduates available to serve as instructors in regional and local archaeological resource protection training.

• SAA should request state historic preservation officers to work with state and local law enforcement agencies to develop archaeological resource protection training for state and local personnel.

• Federal agency managers should provide archaeological resource protection awareness training programs for all employees, concessionaires, contractors, permittees, and other user groups.

• Federal agencies should keep abreast of developments in the area of paleontological resource protection and address training needs as appropriate.

Interagency Cooperation

The goal of the Interagency Cooperation Task Group (Jonathan Dover, chair, Cheryl Munson, recorder) was to promote coordination and cooperation between agencies involved in the protection of archaeological resources and the investigation of archaeological violations through the use of memoranda of understanding, task forces, cross delegations, and the establishment of a national intelligence database. This group identified four recommended actions:

• SAA should support special funding for interagency ARPA operations.

- SAA should strongly support the need for long-term ARPA undercover investigations.
- SAA should sponsor specialized ARPA training for archaeologists not working for the federal government.
- SAA should recommend that federal agencies create a nationwide database for memoranda of understanding and cooperative agreements so that prototypes could be used by any requester to develop agreements allowing law enforcement agencies and prosecutors to further archaeological resource protection.

Information Sharing

The goal of the Information Sharing Task Group (Anne Rogers, chair, Tom Des Jean, recorder) was to identify ways to optimize protection of archaeological resources through three types of proactive information sharing: information sharing within agencies, interagency information sharing, and information sharing between federal agencies and outside entities. This group developed 11 recommendations:

- SAA should urge its membership and other resource preservation organizations to support implementation of the Save the Past for the Future conference recommendations by the U.S. Congress and associated government agencies.
- SAA should support the use of the National Incident Based Reporting System (NIBRS) for tracking ARPA investigations and its use in the secretary of the interior's annual report to Congress under Section 13 of ARPA. Each agency unit should identify a contact person to protect confidentiality and to facilitate agency interaction.
- SAA should support the establishment of line authority reporting procedures for all land management agencies, similar to those currently in use by the Forest Service.
- SAA should support the establishment and funding of ad hoc, case-specific regional task forces, which would develop protocols for information sharing, as well as objectives related to specific cases. Protocols should emphasize that agencies are encouraged to provide information to other agencies where applicable, and that information concerning completed cases should be submitted to the NPS LOOT database.
- SAA should encourage agencies to improve the intra- and interagency flow of information between agency specialists including archaeologists, law enforcement personnel, and attorneys. ARPA terminology should be used to standardize descriptions.
- SAA should urge land management agencies to share the results of ARPA prosecutions with other agencies and with the public.
- SAA should promote agency participation in the LOOT database.
- SAA should develop a site damage assessment training program for its membership.
- SAA should recommend that all federal land management agencies be advised of the ARPA related support available through the NPS Archaeological Assistance Division.
- SAA should sponsor regional information sharing workshops for law enforcement personnel and archaeologists.
- SAA should provide a forum at its annual meeting where archaeologists, law enforcement officers, and attorneys would meet to share information.

Investigative Technologies

The goals of this group (Paul Berkowitz, chair, Susan Morton, recorder) were to identify existing law enforcement technologies that are currently used in ARPA investigations, to assess their effectiveness, and to propose new investigative strategies and technologies to enhance the capability of law enforcement agencies to protect archaeological resources. This group formulated 13 recommendations (1–10, short term; 11–13, long term):

- SAA should develop a position statement in support of law enforcement.
- SAA should seek private funding sources for research and development of technical investigative equipment.
- SAA should adopt a position statement acknowledging Department of Defense contributions to resource protection.
- SAA should compile a list of archaeological forensic resources and make this list available to law enforcement personnel.
- Federal agencies should develop interagency standardization of technical investigative centers and coordinators.
- Federal agencies should promote interagency standardization of technical investigative equipment and training.
- Federal agencies should consider legal issues related to the use of technical investigative equipment, specifically Section 106 of the National Historic Preservation Act, as well as any other relevant legal authorities.
- Federal agencies should develop secure interagency electronic mail systems.
- Federal agencies should explore expanded use of existing laboratories, such as Los Alamos National Laboratory and the NPS Technical Preservation Center, for archaeological forensics and law enforcement technical research and development.
- Federal agencies should explore the use of digital imaging technology for archaeological and law enforcement applications.
- SAA should consider maintaining funding and administrative capabilities for research and development and special equipment acquisitions.
- Federal agencies should ensure that any law enforcement communications and NIBRS systems developed have full interagency interface capabilities.
- Federal agencies should support cooperative interagency development of an ARPA intelligence database or use of an existing intelligence database for this purpose.

Most Significant Recommendations

The Law Enforcement workshop as a whole identified what were considered by group consensus to be the seven highest priority recommendations for actions by SAA or, in one instance, DOJ. (Some priority recommendations were developed independently by more than one task group.) In order of priority, they are:

- SAA should develop a position statement in support of law enforcement.
- SAA should urge its membership and other resource preservation organizations to support implementation of the Save the Past for the Future conference recommendations by the U.S. Congress and associated government agencies.
- SAA should support special funding for interagency ARPA operations.
- SAA should develop a site damage assessment training program for its membership.
- DOJ should transfer ARPA and NAGPRA prosecutions to their Lands and Resources Section where other resource cases are handled currently.
- SAA should request state historic preservation officers to work with state and local law enforcement agencies to develop archaeological resource protection training for state and local personnel.
- SAA should propose to the U.S. Sentencing Commission that it adopt

specific guidelines for ARPA sentencing.

Conclusions

Four conclusion are drawn from the efforts of the Law Enforcement Workshop at the 1994 working conference. First, archaeological resources everywhere in the United States continue to be in great danger of damage or destruction from looting and vandalism.

Second, while many positive steps have been taken to protect archaeological resources, much remains to be accomplished if these resources are to be effectively preserved and protected as an integral part of our national heritage now and in the future.

Third, a number of important recommendations made by two workshops at the 1989 working conference—Combating the Problem and Understanding the Problem—have yet to be acted on or require additional action; these should receive immediate attention by SAA.

Fourth, implementation of the seven priority recommendations developed by the 1994 Law Enforcement Workshop, as well as some or all of the other recommendations developed by the five law enforcement task groups, would significantly enhance law enforcement efforts to protect archaeological resources from looting and vandalism.

PARTICIPANTS

Craig Altop
Department of Geography and Earth Resources
Utah State University
Logan

Roger Anyon
Zuni Heritage and Historic Preservation Office
Zuni, New Mexico

Barto Arnold
State Marine Archaeologist
Society for Historical Archaeology
Texas Historical Commission
Austin

Elizabeth Baquedano
Instituto de Investigaciones Historicas
Ciudad Universita
Mexico City

Pat Barker
Bureau of Land Management
Reno, Nevada

Susan Bender
Department of Sociology and Anthropology
Skidmore College
Saratoga Springs, New York

Judith Bense
Department of Anthropology
University of West Florida
Pensacola

Paul Berkowitz
National Park Service
Herndon, Virginia

Anthony Bonanno
Ranger Activities
National Park Service
Santa Fe, New Mexico

June Boynton
Bureau of Indian Affairs
Portland, Oregon

Michael Boynton
Columbia River Gorge National Scenic Area
Forest Service
U.S. Department of Agriculture
Hood River, Oregon

Randall Bramer
Office of General Counsel
U.S. Department of Agriculture
Boise, Idaho

Richard Brook
Division of Cultural Heritage
Bureau of Land Management
Washington, D.C.

Robert Brunswig, Jr.
Department of Anthropology
University of Northern Colorado
Greely

James Bruseth
Director of Antiquities Protection
Texas Historical Commission
Austin

Laurie Bryant
Bureau of Land Management
Casper, Wyoming

Leonard Burch
Southern Ute Tribe
Ignasious, Colorado

William Butler
Interagency Archeological Services Division
National Park Service
Denver, Colorado

Cathy Cameron
Advisory Council on Historic Preservation
Golden, Colorado

Darrell Cauley
Environmental and Planning Coordination
Bureau of Reclamation
Denver, Colorado

Jo Clark
Western Governors Association
Denver, Colorado

Joelle Clark
Science and Mathematics Learning Center
Northern Arizona University
Flagstaff

Roger Clark
Grand Canyon Trust
Flagstaff, Arizona

Susan Collins
State Archaeologist
Colorado Historical Society
Denver

Dale Davidson
San Juan Resource Area
Bureau of Land Management
Monticello, Utah

Clay Davis
Office of General Counsel
Tennessee Valley Authority
Knoxville

Hester Davis
State Archeologist
Arkansas Archeological Society
Fayetteville

Peter Deane
Nez Perce National Forest
White Bird, Idaho

Ron DeAngelo
Ranger Activities
National Park Service
Philadelphia, Pennsylvania

Evan DeBloois
Forest Service
U.S. Department of Agriculture
Washington, D.C.

Daphne Derven
California Academy of Sciences
San Francisco

Tom Des Jean
Big South Fork National River and Recreation Area
National Park Service
Oneida, Tennessee

John Diefenback
Big South Fork National River and Recreation Area
National Park Service
Oneida, Tennessee

E. James Dixon
Department of Anthropology
Denver Museum of Natural History
Denver, Colorado

Richard Dougherty
Bureau of Land Management
Santa Fe, New Mexico

Amy Douglass
Tempe Historical Museum
Tempe, Arizona

Jonathan Dover
Chaco Protection Sites Program
Navajo Nation
Window Rock, Arizona

Ann Early
Arkansas Archeological Survey
Arkadelphia

Carol Ellick
Statistical Research
Tucson, Arizona

Elizabeth Estill
Forest Service
U.S. Department of Agriculture
Lakewood, Colorado

Brian Fagan
Department of Anthropology
University of California
Santa Barbara

Ed Friedman
Lands, Recreation, and Cultural Resources Branch
Bureau of Reclamation
Denver, Colorado

Daniel Fromstein
Criminal Division
U.S. Department of Justice
Washington, D.C.

Allen Funkhouser
Forest Service
U.S. Department of Agriculture
Silver City, New Mexico

Patrick Garrow
Garrow & Associates
Atlanta, Georgia

Paul Gleeson
Olympic National Park
National Park Service
Port Angeles, Washington

Robert Gough
Natural and Cultural Rights Protection
Rosebud Sioux Tribe
Rosebud, South Dakota

Michael Graves
Department of Anthropology
University of Hawaii
Honolulu

Marlesa Gray
Gray & Pape
Cincinnati, Ohio

Robert Grenier
Marine Archaeology
Ottawa, Ontario

Daniel Haas
Archeological Assistance Division
National Park Service
Washington, D.C.

Chuck Haines
Haskell Indian Nations University
Lawrence, Kansas

Paul Hallam
CEHP Incorporated
Washington, D.C.

Richard Hanes
Bureau of Land Management
Portland, Oregon

Herrick Hanks
Bureau of Land Management
Susanville, California

Donald Hardesty
Department of Anthropology
University of Nevada
Reno

Nancy Hawkins
Division of Archaeology
Office of Cultural Development/SHPO
Baton Rouge, Louisiana

Margaret Heath
Heritage Education Program
Bureau of Land Management
Delores, Colorado

A. Gwynn Henderson
Program for Cultural Resource Assessment
University of Kentucky
Lexington

Teresa Hoffman
Bureau of Reclamation
Phoenix, Arizona

Virginia Horak
Interagency Archeological Services Division
National Park Service
Atlanta, Georgia

John Isaacson
Tri-Services Cultural Resource Research
Center
USA CERL
Champaign, Illinois

Cecil Ison
Daniel Boone National Forest
Forest Service
U.S. Department of Agriculture
Winchester, Kentucky

Calvin Jennings
Department of Anthropology
Colorado State University
Fort Collins

Ralph Johnson
Society for American Archaeology
Washington, D.C.

Cam Jones
Office of the U.S. Attorney General
Memphis, Tennessee

Elwood (Woody) Jones
Federal Law Enforcement Training Center
Forest Service
U.S. Department of Agriculture
Glynco, Georgia

Michael Kaczor
Soil Conservation Service
Washington, D.C.

Ann Kaupp
Department of Anthropology
Smithsonian Institution
Washington, D.C.

Jeffrey Kent
United States Attorney's Office
Eugene, Oregon

Ron King
University of Nevada
Bureau of Land Management
Sparks, Nevada

Keith Kintigh
Department of Anthropology
Arizona State University
Tempe

Timothy Kohler
Department of Anthropology
Washington State University
Pullman

Dorothy Schlotthauer Krass
Archaeological Services
University of Massachusetts
Amherst

Meggett Lavin
National Trust for Historic Preservation
Drayton Hall
Charleston, South Carolina

William Lees
Historic Sites Division
Oklahoma Historical Society
Oklahoma City

Shereen Lerner
Department of Cultural Science
Mesa College
Mesa, Arizona

Kelly Letts
Bureau of Land Management
Salt Lake City, Utah

Fred Limp
Center for Advances Spatial Technology
University of Arkansas
Fayetteville

Bill Lipe
Department of Anthropology
Washington State University
Pullman

Tom Lister
Forest Service
U.S. Department of Agriculture
Payson, Arizona

Jack Lobdell
University of New Mexico
Placitas, New Mexico

Arthur Lunkley, Jr.
Bureau of Land Management
Boise, Idaho

Patrick Lyng
Federal Law Enforcement Training Center
Forest Service
U.S. Department of Agriculture
Glynco, Georgia

Mark Lynott
Midwest Archeological Center
National Park Service
Lincoln, Nebraska

Douglas MacCleery
Forest Inventory, Planning, and Ecology
Forest Service
U.S. Department of Agriculture
Alexandria, Virginia

Cathy MacDonald
Father Leo J. Austin Catholic Secondary School
Port Perry, Ontario

Larry Mackey
United States Attorney's Office
Indianapolis, Indianapolis

Robert Marriott
Ranger Activities
National Park Service
Washington, D.C.

Manny Martinez
Forest Service
U.S. Department of Agriculture
Albuquerque, New Mexico

Martin McAllister
Archaeological Resource Investigations
Duluth, Minnesota

Dennis McLane
Bureau of Land Management
Boise, Idaho

Francis McManamon
Archeological Assistance Division
National Park Service
Washington, D.C.

Phyllis Messenger
Institute of International Studies
Minneapolis, Minnesota

Ronald Michael
Department of Social Sciences
California University of Pennsylvania
California, Pennsylvania

Paul Minnis
Department of Anthropology
University of Oklahoma
Norman

Beverly Mitchum
Pennsylvania Historical and Museum Commission
Harrison City

Jeanne Moe
Bureau of Land Management
Salt Lake City, Utah

John Montgomery
Agency for Conservation Archaeology
Eastern New Mexico University
Portales

Rick Moore
Grand Canyon Trust
Flagstaff, Arizona

James Moriarty
Stanislaus National Forest
Forest Service
U.S. Department of Agriculture
Groveland, California

Wayne Morrissey
Science Policy Research Division
Congressional Research Service
Washington, D.C.

Susan Morton
Archeological Assistance Division
National Park Service
Anchorage, Alaska

Cheryl Munson
Department of Anthropology
Indiana University
Bloomington

Loretta Neumann
CEHP Incorporated
Washington, D.C.

Marilyn Nickels
Division of Cultural Heritage
Bureau of Land Management
Washington, D.C.

Connie Nobles
Department of Education
Southeast Louisiana University
Hammond

Rob Nurre
Acorn Land Resources
Stevens Point, Wisconsin

Jill Osborn
Forest Service
U.S. Department of Agriculture
Washington, D.C.

Felice Pace
Klamath Forest Alliance
Etna, California

David Pendergast
Department of New World Archaeology
Royal Ontario Museum
Toronto, Ontario

Gordon Peters
Superior National Forest
Forest Service
U.S. Department of Agriculture
Duluth, Minnesota

Martin Phillips
Law Enforcement
Bureau of Land Management
Salt Lake City, Utah

David Pokotylo
Canadian Archaeological Association
Department of Anthropology and Sociology
University of British Columbia
Vancouver

Judith Propper
Forest Service
U.S. Department of Agriculture
Albuquerque, New Mexico

Anne Pyburn
Center for Archaeology in the Public Interest
Department of Anthropology
Indiana University
Indianapolis

Constance Ramirez
Environmental Programs Directorate
U.S. Army
Washington, D.C.

Judy Reed
Resources Protection Unit
National Park Service
Santa Fe, New Mexico

John Rick
Department of Anthropology
Stanford University
Stanford, California

Bruce Rippeteau
South Carolina Institute of Archaeology
Columbia

Anne Rogers
Department of Geosciences and Anthropology
Western Carolina University
Cullowhee, North Carolina

James Rogers
Bureau of Land Management
Roswell, New Mexico

Kristine Olson Rogers
Office of the United States Attorney
Portland, Oregon

Jill Schaefer
CEHP Incorporated
Washington, D.C.

Lynell Schalk
Bureau of Land Management
Portland, Oregon

Kathleen Schamel
CEHP Incorporated
Washington, D.C.

Douglas Scott
Lincoln, Nebraska

Donna Seifert
John Milner Associates
Alexandria, Virginia

Ruth Selig
Office of the Assistant Secretary for Science
Smithsonian Institution
Washington, D.C.

Robert Simmons
Office of General Counsel
Forest Service
U.S. Department of Agriculture

Katherine Slick
National Trust for Historic Preservation
Las Vegas, New Mexico

Karolyn Smardz
Toronto Historical Board
Toronto, Ontario

Bruce Smith
Department of Anthropology
Smithsonian Institution
Washington, D.C.

George Smith
Southeast Archeological Center
National Park Service
Tallahassee, Florida

KC Smith
Museum of Florida History
Tallahassee, Florida

Shelley Smith
Bureau of Land Management
Salt Lake City, Utah

Dean Snow
Department of Anthropology
University at Albany, SUNY
Albany, New York

Mary Spearing
Criminal Division
U.S. Department of Justice

Roderick (Rick) Sprague
Laboratory of Anthropology
University of Idaho
Moscow

Barbara Stark
Department of Anthropology
Arizona State University
Tempe

Michael Sweeney
Office of the Secretary of the Interior
Department of the Interior
Washington, D.C.

Erv Taylor
Radiocarbon Laboratory
University of California
Riverside

Paul Thies
Conservation Branch
U.S. Army Environmental Center
Aberdeen Proving Ground, Maryland

Roderick Thornton
Federal Law Enforcement Training Center
Forest Service
U.S. Department of Agriculture
Glynco, Georgia

Al Tonetti
Ohio Historic Preservation Office
Columbus

Ole Varmer
Office of Assistant General Counsel for Ocean Services
National Oceanic and Atmospheric Administration
Silver Spring, Maryland

Patricia (Pam) Wheat
Crow Canyon Archaeological Center
Cortez, Colorado

Nancy White
Department of Anthropology
University of South Florida
Tampa, Florida

Joyce Williams
Office of Contract Archaeology
Southern Illinois University
Edwardsville

Martha Williams
Public Education and Information Committee
Society for Historical Archaeology
Falls Church, Virginia

Kate Winthrop
Bureau of Land Management
Medford, Oregon

Renata Wolynec
Department of Sociology, Anthropology, and Social Work
Edinboro University of Pennsylvania
Edinboro, Pennsylvania

S. Rigby Wright
Manti-LaSal National Forest
Monticello, Utah

Andrew Yatsko
Natural Resources Office
NAS North Island
San Diego, California

Phillip Young
Resource Protection Task Force
National Park Service
Santa Fe, New Mexico

Sandra Zacharias
Deva Heritage Consulting
Vancouver, British Columbia

NOTES

NOTES